M000230199

"The Gate-Crasher knew what lay before him: He must descent into hell and pull the devil's teeth. It was Clyde Barrow versus Fort Knox. Roseanne versus Denny's page three. Wearing a blue blazer and a tie, Albert Einstein's haircut and glasses on the end of his pointy nose, Rich set off to penetrate the most impenetrable fortress in U.S. history.

"The fortress lost. Rich was inside in six minutes. I followed him the whole way. It was pure art.

"Memo to NFL Commissioner Paul Tagliabue: $7 million in security wasn't enough. Memo to Salt Lake Olympic Committee: He'll be there this week."

— Rick Reilly
Sports Illustrated
Talking about Dion at
Super Bowl XXXVI

"The tales of real life adventure with a man who is at ease with kings, sports stars, Hollywood actresses, strippers, gamblers, TV celebrities, and Bankers. Dion's world is one of excitement, flash, and show biz but beneath that man about town outward veneer, there is a man devoted to his country. It's all here in his exciting world as a man who has crashed more events and caused much grief to those in the Academy Awards, the Super Bowl, and World Series than any man alive. Truly a man who enjoys life to the fullest."

— Jerry Gross
Sports Director KPRZ

"It's hard to imagine anyone able to catch up with or who could corral Dion Rich. The nation's political, sports, and entertainment shrines have been penetrated by this 'shadow.'

"Officials involved with the last Super Bowl in San Diego finally found a way. They went to his home, escorted him to the game and made sure he purchased a ticket. Otherwise, the world has been his stage and the astonished actors shared it with this canny intruder.

"Arguably, Dion has been America's guest even thought his name hasn't appeared on registration lists.

"Remarkable guy. Needless to say, his life has been chock-full of surprises."

— Johnny McDonald
Writer and author

"It's a pleasure for me to recommend *Confessions of the World's Greatest Gate-Crasher*. This is the story of a man who, without any doubt, has the deserved national reputation of being tops in his field. Dion Rich has packed more fun and drama into his life than any ten other people I know. Dion and co-author Charlie Jones capture the feel of the excitement of the planning and the skills required to be in the middle of some of this nation's largest events, without invitation. To put it simply, Dion Rich, the greatest gate-crasher of his time, is a kick! Read on. Look at the pictures and learn how he does it with a wink and a smile."

— Fred Lewis
TV host and creator of the
Heart of San Diego

"Dion Rich would be no less than even-money against the U.S. Mint. He's a Houdini when it comes to showing up at places without bothering to purchase a ticket, and he does it with such class, such humor. An artist, clearly."

— Jerry Magee
San Diego Union-Tribune

"There can be no doubt when the *Gate-Crashers Hall of Fame* is finally established; Dion will be a unanimous first choice for induction. Combining guile, boldness, chutzpah, and intelligence Dion has made attending every type of major event without a ticket seem way too easy. Over the years he has accomplished what many of us only dream about doing. His research and game planning prior to every event is the envy of Super Bowl-winning head football coaches. The book is fun for all of us ordinary people and can serve as a great resource for anyone thinking of following in Dion's footsteps."

— Coach Tom Bass
Writer, poet, lecturer
NFL Defensive Coordinator

"There are hundreds of imposters; however, there is only one real imposter, Dion Rich! A story that is hard to believe, but absolutely true."

— Bob Shumake
Retired advertising executive

"IF YOU DON'T KNOW DION RICH, life has tossed you a curve. This lovable character is what movies are made of and, if Hollywood passes him by, shame on them."

— Chuck Di Rocco
Editor and Publisher of *Gaming Today*

"Dion Rich is San Diego's James Bond: Suave, debonair, cunning . . . and he doesn't pay for his own martinis. Dion has brass balls and a heart of gold. Reading his secrets about gate-crashing is like stealing home in slow motion."

— Bill Swank
Baseball Historian, Author,
Echoes from Lane Field and
Baseball in San Diego

"Extraordinary guy and extraordinary story."

— Rick Smith
NFL Retired

"Better storyteller than Casey Stengel."

— Paul Mendes
International soccer promoter

Confessions of the
World's
Greatest
Gate-Crasher:
DION RICH

CHARLIE JONES

SEVEN LOCKS PRESS

Santa Ana, California

Confessions of the World's Greatest Gate-Crasher: Dion Rich © 2003 by Charlie Jones. All rights reserved. Printed in the United States of America. No part of this book may be used or reproduced in any manner whatsoever without written permission except in the case of reprints in the context of reviews. For information, write Seven Locks Press, 3100 W. Warner Ave., #8, Santa Ana, California 92704.

Library of Congress Cataloging-in-Publication Data is available from the publisher.
ISBN 1-931643-24-5   Paper
ISBN 1-931643-25-3   Hardcover

Book design by Heather Buchman

"The crasher in the new millennium will have to be very high-tech oriented. New gadgetry and electronic security will make a typical crash a lot more difficult and time-consuming."

— Dion Rich

Dedication

To my Mom, Dad, and Pat—
three of the most influential people in my life—
with love.

— Dion

Acknowledgements

Special thanks to the late Bob Sterling, Bill Randall, Nick Canepa, Bill Swank, Chuck Di Rocco, and Rick Reilly.

Foreword

NICK CANEPA
SPORTS COLUMNIST
San Diego Union-Tribune

Dion Rich is no longer the NFL's Number One Enemy. But he used to be. For more than twenty years, the NFL "secret police" chased the world's greatest gate-crasher, although most of the time it was like *The Pink Panther* with Inspector Clouseau trying to catch David Niven. By the time the NFL finally caught up with the slippery Rich, he already had far more than his fifteen minutes of fame.

For Rich, it has always been more than crashing a gate. When it came to Super Bowls, it was a matter of getting on the field during the game, getting his picture taken with the winning coach, and getting into the winning locker room. Then there was his appetite for inclusion in TV shots or inclusion in award ceremony photographs.

Don't laugh. It's all about being documented, and many of Rich's exploits have been written about or photographed. There is a great picture of him carrying Tom Landry off the field after a Super Bowl win. There's a famous one of him standing on the podium in the Green Bay locker room with Vince Lombardi as he accepts the trophy from Pete Rozelle after Super Bowl I, plus many more.

The NFL had been after Rich for years, but Dion was too crafty. "For Super Bowl XXIII in Miami, I wore a disguise and had an accomplice pushing me around in a wheelchair," Rich recalls. "It's the only game ever where I didn't stand for the national anthem. They caught me just as I was getting ready to go into the locker room and get my picture taken with Eddie DeBartolo. A sergeant on Miami's police department came up to me and said, "Dion, you're out of here."

One thing about the NFL, it never got mad enough at Dion to have him arrested, which no doubt it could have done.

Dion Rich is not out to beat someone out of the price of a ticket. He's a lover of good food and equally good company, with the financial wherewithal to live the life of an adventurer who loves to be around celebrities and is generous to a fault. People don't realize that he takes a group of fifty handicapped kids to San Diego Padres' baseball games annually and is involved in innumerable humanitarian and civic activities in San Diego.

Dion and his kids at a Padres game

It's just that he's known as "The Crasher"—maybe the greatest the world has ever seen. And while Super Bowl crashing is what made him famous, he's crashed Olympics, both Summer and Winter, World Series, All-Star games (MLB and NBA), championship fights, Breeders Cup, America's Cup in Australia and San Diego, and the Kentucky Derby. He's also crashed major events such as the Academy Awards' ceremony and its post-event Governor's Ball, the Emmys, Golden Globes, SAG awards, and the Playboy Mansion, to mention a few.

Dion's in it for the rush. Most times he has tickets to an event, but crashes for the pure thrill of it. If he gets thrown out, he just turns around and goes right back in, another way.

"Out of all the Super Bowls that have been played, I've crashed all but two. The first was Super Bowl III because I was off skiing," says Dion. "The other was Super Bowl XXXVII, and that was because I was escorted *in* (yes, *in!*) by the San Diego police and the Justice Department."

"Skill is involved, but you have to be lucky, too. And, of course, being experienced helps lower the odds. As in life, timing and luck are an integral segment of crashing."

He misses those days of getting on the field, but he realizes they're over. "I don't get the urge, though, not really," he says. "I'm kind of like a retired ballplayer who's over the hill and fantasizes that he can still do it but knows he can't."

So he won't crash the gate of the next Super Bowl, right? "Oh, I'll have a ticket, but I just might try to crash the gate," he says. "That's automatic. I've never been caught trying to crash a Super Bowl gate. Ever."

It's doubtful that his streak will ever be broken.

Prologue

HOW TO BE A GATE-CRASHER

"It takes a little skill, a lot of luck, a lot of timing,

plus lots of desire, hard work, connections, intestinal fortitude,

and ice water in your veins. If there's such a thing as reincarnation,

I just might come back as a burglar."

— Dion Rich

IN THE BEGINNING

My football "crashing" actually began at Balboa Stadium back in the old American Football League days when the San Diego Chargers moved down the coast from Los Angeles in 1961. I was such a regular on the Chargers' bench that my nickname among the players was "Splinters" (for sliding up and down the bench).

After one game in which Denver kicked the Chargers' butt big time, head coach Sid Gilman stomped over to me in the locker room, waggled his finger in my face, and shouted that he never wanted to see me on the bench again. So from then on, I went over to the other side and sat on the visitors' bench.

The last time I was on the field for a Chargers game was in 1972 with Detroit. A good friend of mine, Chuck Knox, former head coach of the L.A. Rams and Buffalo Bills, then an assistant coach with the Detroit Lions, gave me a sidelines' credential. Not more than ten minutes into the first quarter, the late Irv Kaze, then Chargers' business manager, spotted me. He screamed at his assistant, "Get Dion off the field!" ending a nice tenure on the sidelines. This was not a deterrent, however, to my converging on the L.A. Rams' sidelines in later years when my close friend, Ray Malavasi, was head coach, or in September of 1992, my riding on the L.A. Raiders' team plane to play Cincinnati. Cincinnati won in overtime twenty-four to twenty-one.

"Crashes"

Chapter One

SUPER BOWL XII
JANUARY 15, 1978
NEW ORLEANS SUPERDOME
DALLAS COWBOYS 27 – DENVER BRONCOS 10
Provided a memorable Kodak moment.

After eleven years of playing cat and mouse with NFL security, it became exceedingly more difficult to "crash" the field at the Super Bowl without being detected. This particular year, 1978, credentials were at a premium and what appeared to be an audacious, seemingly impossible situation, turned into an unprecedented entrance onto the field.

Red Miller, then head coach of the Denver Broncos and a personal friend of mine since his early days as an assistant coach at Denver, gave me the okay to ride into the New Orleans Superdome on the team bus. Talk about luck. This was my day. The only uneasiness I encountered was when I ended up sitting directly behind the NFL security officials on the bus. But I was able to keep my usual low profile, and they didn't notice me.

When I got off the team bus, I walked directly into the locker room, and from there I walked right onto the field with the players. I found a nice spot where there was a small crowd of people—where I wouldn't stand out. And I stayed there.

One of my many secrets is to stay in one place and not look conspicuous. As Super Bowls went by over time, it became exceedingly difficult, if not impossible, to avoid the NFL's all-seeing eye. They learned my true identity and prominently displayed my photo.

It was late in the fourth quarter of Super Bowl XII when I realized Denver didn't have a prayer of winning the game. At that moment, my thoughts, but not my sentiment, turned toward the Cowboys. I knew I was a traitor—I admit it—but something had to be done. Knowing time was of the essence and the two-minute warning would soon be sounded, I cautiously moved toward Tom Landry's side of the field. Every time the ball was snapped, I inched closer to the Dallas side. The key is moving only when the ball is in play because that's when everyone is watching the game. They aren't looking for someone moving cautiously around the field. It didn't take me long to place myself right in the middle of the Cowboys' bench.

I hadn't thought of it until then, but I suddenly decided to do something I'd never done before. At the end of each game, I always got as close to the winning head coach as I could, to get a shot on television or in the newspapers or in some national magazine. It occurred to me that it would be really great to get the winning coach up on my shoulder.

I edged closer and closer. I kept one eye on the clock and one eye on Tom Landry. The last minute started ticking down. I kept moving closer and closer, and BOOM! Dallas defensive tackle Larry Cole and I grabbed him at exactly the same time, and the cameras clicked away.

I never had any idea how famous that picture would become. When Landry passed away, it was on the front page of the Austin newspaper. It was in many papers all over the world and in the Pro Football Hall of Fame in Canton, Ohio. In fact, it became one of the most famous pictures in the history of the NFL.

Now comes the irony. Not more than a few seconds after making my grab, Denver head coach Red Miller, who made my "crash" possible, came running across the field to congratulate his opposition. And guess who he sees on my shoulder? You got it—his opposition, Tom Landry!

It was one of those once-in-a-lifetime scenes, to be standing face-to-face with both the winning and the losing Super Bowl XII head coaches, right there in the middle of the Superdome at the end of the game. It was one of my greatest moments in gate-crashing!

Red's mouth dropped open in complete amazement. He looked at me like he was thinking, "Dion, what the hell is going on?" Then his look turned to a big grin once he realized what I was up to, and we exited laughing.

RETURN TO GLORY

I was back in New Orleans for Super Bowl XXXVI when Rick Reilly, who is one of sports most accomplished writers (authors the "Back Page" column for *Sports Illustrated*), asked me to show him how I "crash" a Super Bowl. His intent was to trail along.

He timed me. I was in, in six minutes. I would have been in sooner but I stopped for a few minutes to take photos outside the Dome. I thought it might be my last photo opportunity before being incarcerated for life. You never know how serious the NFL has become.

There was a small passageway, about a foot between the people who were entering the metal detector and the fence. I waited until the crowd started in, then edged through the passageway. Looking around, I saw an unguarded side door that just happened to be open, and BINGO . . .

Rick was really impressed.

Sports Illustrated columnist Rick Reilly learns how to "crash." It's an official "crash" if the ticket is not torn!

In Like Flynn
by Rick Reilly

COMING TO the Big Easy, 72-year-old Dion Rich had sneaked, weaseled, conned, bluffed, tricked and bam-boozled his way into 32 straight Super Bowls, the record for a man refusing to touch his wallet.

Wait. Not just into the games, but often onto the fields and into the locker rooms. That's Rich on the winner's podium with Vince Lombardi and Pete Rozelle after the first Super Bowl. That's him helping to carry Cowboys coach Tom Landry off the field after XII. That's him whispering sweet nothings into coach Joe Gibbs's ear as the Redskins run off after winning XVII.

Wait, wait. It's not only Super Bowls, Rich has gone ticketless into World Series games, title fights, America's Cup races, Kentucky Derbies and 14 Olympics. Basically, he's Red Smith without the deadlines. He's also crashed eight Academy Awards, as proved by pictures like the one of him with his arm around Gwyneth Paltrow after she won her Oscar. He even has a snap of himself at the Playboy Mansion, in Hugh Hefner's bathrobe.

It's not that Rich is poor. He's made boatloads in real estate and other things. "But why pay when you don't have to?" he asks.

Then came Super Bowl XXXVI, hard on the heels of 9/11. The NFL spent $7 million on a mammoth security effort manned by the Secret Service, the FBI, FEMA, the National Guard, U.S. Marshals and dozens of state and local law-enforcement agencies. The week looked bleak for the Sneak Streak.

It got worse. Everywhere Rich looked, there were Jeeps, Humvees and even tanks. There were more wands around than at a fairy godmother convention. Security was triple anything he had seen before. A 10-foot-high chain-link-and-barbed-wire fence was put up around the perimeter of the Louisiana Superdome.

Welcome to the Big Hard.

Dion cased the Superdome and declared it tighter than Joan Rivers's eyelids. How could any of his tricks work? The wheel-chair? Claiming to be a ref? Pretending to be with the team, the band, the stadium crew? The Coke-bottle bifocals? The bag of press credentials? "If every Super Bowl were like this," he sighed in a media center he wasn't supposed to be in last Thursday, "I'd retire."

Not only that, but he was sure he was being followed. The NFL admits it has tailed him. "Oh, yeah, I've heard of him," Milt Ahlerich, the league's vice president of security, grumbled. The NFL once told Rich if it ever caught him on the field again, he'd be finding out if he could sneak out of jail. He agreed to stay off the fields--but he never said anything about stadiums.

A streak is a streak, wartime or peace, and the Gate-Crasher knew what lay before him: He must descent into hell and pull the devil's teeth. It was Clyde Barrow versus Fort Knox. Roseanne versus Denny's page 3. Wearing a blue blazer and a tie, Albert Einstein's haircut and glasses on the end of his pointy nose, Rich set off to penetrate the most impenetrable fortress in U.S. history.

The fortress lost. Rich was inside in six minutes. I followed him the whole way. It was pure art.

He doddered, darted, acted addled and hurried, slunk through tiny spaces and sped through unguarded ones. He was Frogger Senior. He never stopped walking and never started hearing. He nudged his way through the masses at the first security checkpoint and ticket check, waited until a young guard (he always looks for the youngest) had her head buried in a bag, sidestepped past her and through the one-foot gap between the metal detector and a fence. Then he buttonhooked a distracted wand man, did a pirouette around a bored National Guardsman that would've made Fred Astaire weep and then beat it up a ramp. He was never security-screened. Thank God he's on our side.

Now he had to get by the ticket rippers. He found a bank of unmanned doors locked from the inside, waited until a supervisor came barreling out of one, lithely slid his loafer into the gap before it closed and stepped through it as casually as if he were entering his own kitchen. "When am I going to learn never to bet against myself?" he said, grinning.

Make it 33.

Memo to NFL commissioner Paul Tagliabue: $7 million wasn't enough. Memo to Salt Lake Olympic Committee: He'll be there this week.

I didn't hear from Dion again until midnight. He called from inside the Rams' postgame party, gobbling free gumbo and sipping gratis merlot. Hey, at least they had one winner in there.

PHOTO OPPORTUNITY

In addition to crashing high profile sports events, I also love to collect photos of me with high profile personalities. One of my favorites is with Tony Bennett. It took place in the men's room at the Golden Globes in Los Angeles.

I asked, "Tony, can I get a shot?" He said, "Sure." I handed my camera to some guy who was standing there. But, I did wait until after Tony had washed his hands.

Cleaning up with Tony Bennett

RULES OF THE GAME

A photograph is the best evidence that you actually completed your "crash" and that it was official.

DION SAYS:

"They are all small potatoes compared to the Super Bowl.

That's the **BIG ONE.**

That's the **CHALLENGE.** *"*

KEYS TO CRASHING

Dress the part.

Move slowly but quickly.

Adopt the attitude that you belong there.

Chapter Two

***

ACADEMY AWARDS
MARCH 21, 1999
DOROTHY CHANDLER PAVILION, LOS ANGELES
Holding an Oscar and an Oscar winner.

When you're watching the Oscars on television, virtually every seat in the theater is filled when the commercial break is over. This is due to professional seat fillers who literally stand in readiness to fill vacant seats. Men in tuxes stand in one line, with women in formal gowns in another. As soon as a seat is vacated, the supervisor, holding a clipboard, says, "Okay, there are two seats over there, four seats here, one seat down front," and the fillers immediately go to the empty seats.

The fillers all have a number on a chain around their necks. When seated, they move the number around to their back. This way, the numbers won't be seen on camera, but the supervisor and security can easily see where the fillers are sitting.

Once I crash an event, I like to snoop around and see what kind of additional mischief I can get into. At one of my early Oscar ceremonies, I happened to end up in this room crowded with seat fillers. Upon learning what they were doing, I figured I might as well join them and become a professional seat filler myself. Thus, when they walked in, I walked right in with them and found a seat down front.

At the 1999 Academy Awards, I got a seat in the fourth row by this method, but there also happened to be three empty seats to my left. This was noticeable and I think brought the heat on me.

A quick flashback is required here to show you how I had expected it to work: For the Emmys one year, I was in the fifth row and this guy got up from about the ninth row. He was African-American and had just been announced as recipient of the Emmy for Best Director for *NYPD Blues*. I stood up, put my arms around him, shook his hands, and said, "Great job." Then I went back to my seat. I turned to the woman next to me and asked her if she knew who he was. She exclaimed, "You don't know who he is?!" Then she told me he was Paris Barclay, I said thank you and wrote it down.

This is exactly what I was planning to do at the Academy Awards. I had figured out that if someone behind me won an Oscar, I was going to get up and give them a big hug because the television cameras would zoom right in on the winner and also on me.

Unfortunately, it didn't happen that way. I did get on television though because I was sitting directly behind Jack Nicholson and Steven Spielberg. A lot of people saw me but it was just a quick flash. If you weren't looking right at Spielberg's left ear, you wouldn't have seen me. Then all of a sudden two big undercover Los Angeles cops in tuxes walked up and motioned to me (LAPD cops moonlight for the Oscars), and I knew my gig was up.

They escorted me out in front of the entire Academy Awards audience. This would embarrass the normal person, but did I ever represent myself as normal? They took me outside where a female Academy person made some inquiries:

"Where's your ticket?"

"My wife has it."

"Where's your wife?"

"In the ladies' room."

"Where are you supposed to meet her?"

"Right outside the ladies' room."

"Where are you sitting?"

"In the balcony."

"Is your wife a member of the Academy?"

"No." I'm still not missing a beat. "But we're with members of the Academy."

"What are their names?"

"I don't know. They're friends of my wife." This is probably one of the biggest lies I've ever told. I've never been married. Engaged, yes. Married, never.

At this point, they were getting tired of interrogating me. They took my driver's license and got my name, address, telephone number, and Social Security number. They took two police mug shots (front and profile) with my name under my chin, and then they let me go.

At this point, they made a rookie mistake because they did not escort me out past the yellow ribbon that reads, "Police line, do not cross." If they had thrown me out past that yellow ribbon, I could never have gotten into the Governor's Ball that is held right after the Awards ceremony, in the same complex. They threw me out on the red carpet, so I busied myself getting more pictures with celebrities.

After the Academy Awards, it was time to eat, so I crashed the Governor's Ball. I waited inconspicuously until everyone was seated, then spotted a table that was half-empty. I waited even longer until they were halfway through with their meal. At this point, I quietly joined them.

As soon as I sat, a young lady came up to me and inquired, "Sir, would you like to be waited on?"

"Yes, ma'am, I would."

When she asked for my ticket, I made firm eye contact and said with a slight edge, "Ma'am, my wife gave either you or that other waiter our ticket some time ago. After a half-hour wait, she was so P.O.'ed, she left, and I'm not sure if I'll ever see her again!"

Within five minutes, I was eating fresh salmon and filet mignon, medium rare. That salmon was so fresh it tasted like it had jumped mere moments ago from the water into the cooking pan. And the evening

Gwyneth Paltrow—an Oscar hug

continued in that vein. After a good dinner and a little dancing, I polished it off by having my picture taken with Gwyneth Paltrow.

Close to midnight, as I was leaving the Ball with a stack of picture frames and the little bags the Academy provides stuffed with the evening's favors, I literally ran right into the woman who had interrogated me earlier. She confronted me with, "Where's your wife?" I answered, "I'm still looking for her," and continued on my way to crash the other Oscar parties of the evening. Why they didn't throw me out of the Governor's Ball still remains a mystery to this day. I'm still batting a thousand with the Goveror's Ball.

But my Academy experience of that year was not over. Almost two months later, I had the following literary exchange with the executive administrator.

Letter from the Academy of Motion Pictures Arts and Sciences—gold embossed:

May 11, 1999

Dear Mr. Rich:

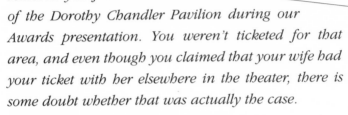

As we reconstruct the evidence, it looks like you had quite a night last March 21st.

First, the Academy security personnel removed you from the orchestra section of the Dorothy Chandler Pavilion during our Awards presentation. You weren't ticketed for that area, and even though you claimed that your wife had your ticket with her elsewhere in the theater, there is some doubt whether that was actually the case.

Later, you were seen (and photographed) inside the Governors Ball, dancing the night away, your pockets bulging with the picture frames that were intended as gifts for our guests at the Ball.

A thorough search of our lists of those invited to the Awards Presentation and the Ball fails to turn up your name anywhere. It's possible, I suppose, that you were someone's guest. If that was the case, I'd appreciate learning the name of that person.

If, on the other hand, you're unable to help us under-stand the basis for your being inside the Chandler and the Ball, then we'll assume that the suspicions of our security experts were correct, that you're a particularly persistent trespasser. It's your move.

Sincerely,

Ric Robertson

Executive Administrator of the Academy of Motion Pictures Arts and Sciences

My rebuttal – Certified mail, return receipt requested:

July 15, 1999

Dear Mr. Robertson:

Please excuse the protracted delay in replying to your correspondence dated May 11, 1999. May I begin by saying that innumerable people in the industry have informed me that the lower segment of the orchestra seats are to be filled ensuing each presentation, which, as you know, is at the commercial break. Much to my dismay, I found you have your own professional seat fillers in which to fulfill your obligation. If you were cognizant of the situation at the aforementioned evening, you would have noticed the three adjacent seats to my left, in the fourth row, directly behind Jack Nicholson and Steven Spielberg, were vacated for a minimum of two to three intermissions, which I felt was not too professional on your part. In paragraph three of your letter, you state, and I quote, "Later, you were seen and photographed inside the Governors Ball, dancing the night away, your pockets bulging with the picture frames that were intended as gifts for our guests at the Ball."

Mr. Robertson, may I say in my own defense, that at all prior Governors Balls I've attended, I've never failed to document an overabundance of memorabilia left behind merely for the waiters and kitchen help to scavenge at the conclusion of your extravaganza. I merely beat the staff to them, and got my Christmas shopping done early. The exquisite little gift bags you provided us for the goodies were quite unique, but I feel next year they should be made even larger.

Now for paragraph four, and getting to the crux of the issue at hand. After learning that I had been so unceremoniously ejected in front of the entire Academy, my wife was so embarrassed and humiliated that she would not confide in me the names of the benevolent couple who so graciously got us into the Awards presentation.

Sincerely and most respectively,

Dion Rich

PS. I greatly appreciate your unparalleled wit and sense of humor.

Second letter from the Academy:

March 20, 2001

Dear Mr. Rich:

It has come to our attention that you may try to enter this year's ACADEMY AWARDS ceremony without invitation or permission from the Academy. While we do not know whether or not this is true, you should be aware that the ACADEMY AWARDS ceremony is a private event and tickets are expressly nontransferable. The OSCAR telecast is one of the most widely watched live television events in the world and, as such, poses a very attractive target to those who might try to disrupt the ceremony in the name of their cause. While we have no reason to believe that disruption is your intent, I'm sure you'll understand why the Academy goes to great lengths to be certain that it knows who exactly is being provided access. Anyone caught at the ceremony in possession of transferred tickets or found to have entered without a ticket, will be treated as a trespasser and prosecuted accordingly.

Very truly yours,

Scott Miller

Assistant Counsel

Postscipt: Later I called Ric Robertson at the Academy and told him how he could improve his security. I also told him I would never darken his door again. (However, that pledge did not apply to the many social events that surround the Academy Awards. I continue to wine and dine with the Oscar winners each year.)

A toast to the Academy

Ed Asner and Lauren Bacall

Superstars: Nicolas Cage and Sean Connery

"The Host" Billy Crystal, and Leonardo DiCaprio

Multi-talented Danny DeVito and Michael Douglas

Thanks for the memories—Bob Hope and Paul Newman; In 1968, I had the pleasure of working with Bob in the "Bob Hope USO Show" at San Diego Stadium.

The pretty and the powerful, Faye Dunaway and Merv Griffin; In 1962, I appeared on Merv's New York show "Play Your Hunch."

Thanks for the memories—Bob Hope and Paul Newman; In 1968, I had the pleasure of working with Bob in the "Bob Hope USO Show" at San Diego Stadium.

The pretty and the powerful, Faye Dunaway and Merv Griffin; In 1962, I appeared on Merv's New York show "Play Your Hunch."

Sarah Jessica Parker, and the one and only, Oprah Winfrey

Nancy Reagan and Joan Rivers

Tom Selleck, and Claudia Schiffer and the magical David Copperfield

Anna Nicole Smith, and Paul and Mira Sorvino

Tom Hanks and Dustin Hoffman—big time Oscar winners

Nicole Kidman and Tom Cruise; Shirley MacLaine

Oscar winners Kevin Spacey and Meryl Streep

John Travolta and Robin Williams

MISTAKEN IDENTITY

This happened at Army Archerd's fiftieth—a gala celebration thrown by *Variety Magazine* at the Beverly Hilton Hotel in Los Angeles. After I crashed the party, I waited until most everyone had finished their salad. Then I spotted a table that had three empty seats. I didn't go down close to the stage. To do that is a rookie mistake.

I sat down. Subsequently, the other two empty seats filled as well. There were a couple of people who looked at the number on the table but, fortunately, they went on and sat elsewhere.

"Him"—Army Archerd

You know you're home free at a table when the waiter takes the number off the table, which he did in about ten minutes. A little while later, the elderly lady on my left said to me, "How long have you known Army?" I replied, "Oh, I've known *her* probably about five or six years. How about you?" She said, "Oh, I've known *him* longer than you would want to!" *Woops!*

FIRST TIME

Mickey Rooney is the first celebrity that I ever asked for an autograph. Back in 1939 when I was nine years old, my aunt and uncle lived on the corner of Century Boulevard and Prairie in Inglewood. This was right across from the Hollywood Park Race Track. They had some big 4th of July function that the family all attended. As we were coming out, everybody said, "There's Mickey Rooney." So I ran across the street and got his autograph. He said, "Kid, watch out for the traffic."

Mickey Rooney and his wife

This was right in the heart of the Depression and my first time ever to see a limo. It was a far cry from the poverty I was accustomed to. I was more familiar with leaky roofs and going to school in old clothes and shoes. Little was I to know that some sixty years later I would have the pleasure of having my picture with "Mickey" at one of the Oscars' more illustrious parties.

HAT TRICK

My show business "hat trick" was being thrown out of the Academy Awards, the Emmys, and the Screen Actors Guild Awards, all by the same security person—LAPD Sergeant Kirk Smith (AKA: Smitty).

Although, admittedly, Smitty can be and has been extremely nice, he did seize my camera at a SAG event and remove film of Halle Berry and Ed Asner. Of course, if I hadn't opened my mouth and admitted to having a camera before entering the metal detector, I would never have been questioned on how I had gained entrance in the first place. His partner, Paul Partridge also of the LAPD, would also not have been able to say, after I had hardly uttered more than a couple of evasive words, "Dion's lying!" I was only fibbing a little to protect the innocent.

Even so, Smitty's final words were not music to my ears:

"Dion, I don't care how many events you crash as long as you don't crash mine. Tell me what three events you'll never crash for the rest of your life."

As I met his eyes, eyeball to eyeball, and uttered the words, "Academy Awards, Emmys, and SAG," my inner voice began to chant longingly: C*old beer, cold beer* . . .

An hour later while driving home, a couple more thoughts came to mind having to do with Smitty: that I would *definitely* stay away from *any* event he had anything to do with!! And that I had forgotten to salute as I exited his presence.

RULES OF THE GAME

It's an official "gate-crash" at a social event as soon as you are inside, without a torn ticket or an official credential, *and* you have eaten and finished one drink of any kind. If you are thrown out in the middle of the meal, it is *not* official.

DION SAYS:

"I know from experience that it feels

WAY *better to be thrown out on a*

FULL *stomach than an* **EMPTY** *one."*

KEYS TO CRASHING

Eat as soon as possible.

When caught, admit your error and exit gracefully.

Don't let being thrown out deter you from trying again.

Chapter Three

ALL-STAR GAMES AND WORLD SERIES
It was the old "Kissing-Your-Sister Tie Trick."

This is the Major League All-Star Game in Atlanta in 2000. I had a pass to get in. The following will show you how the element of connections plays a part in gate-crashing.

I borrowed a credential. I don't want to name the man I got it from because I don't want to get him in trouble. Suffice to say he's with a TV network on the East Coast. This was also before 9/11, so it was easy (9/11, by the way, is a gate-crasher's worst nightmare).

I didn't even have to show any ID. I just went up and gave his name and they gave me his credential. Everything went fine, and I immediately went down on the field.

A borrowed credential is okay. The important thing is what you do once you get in.

From there, I went into the National League clubhouse. Big sign: NO PICTURES ALLOWED. I got a picture with that sign. I got my second picture with Randy Johnson.

They had all these beautiful baseball caps out on the table. I figured the media was entitled to them. I knew I wasn't supposed to take pictures or take a cap, but I thought, *Oh, what the heck, I'm not official media.* And since I had already taken a picture, I decided to take a cap.

I picked one up and put it in my pocket. The clubhouse boy nabbed me as I go out. He said, "You can't have that. They're for the players only."

The Big Unit—Randy Johnson

I said, "I'm terribly sorry." I put it back.

From there, I went in the American League clubhouse to get more pictures. No sooner was I in than the clubhouse boy and one of the officials came in. The official jerked his head towards me and barked, "Is this the guy?" The clubhouse boy nodded, "Yeah, that's the guy." The official turned to me and asked, "Who are you with?"

"East Coast Media."

"Really? You know, you're not supposed to take those caps."

I then found myself being escorted into another room with another official, where we were soon joined by the Atlanta police. Sweat began to trickle down the inside of my shirt.

The new official turned to me with a curt, "Identification."

I handed it over.

"Where'd you get that?"

"I'm working for the media company."

"Really? What's their number?"

"I don't have it with me. I have it at the hotel."

At that point, I was thinking they were going to take me to jail, especially when the cops walked in. But just about the time my shirt was drenched with sweat, they let me go. I immediately called my guy to tell him what was up, as I was afraid he was going to lose his credential for Major League Baseball (luckily, he didn't).

The ultimate result was that I am now on a first name basis with the Atlanta police in addition to the Miami police, San Diego police, San Diego Sheriff's department, LAPD, and eventually the Salt Lake City police department and the Secret Service. They did keep the credential and throw me out. But, believe me, I really was sweatin' it!

Not having anything else to do, I crashed back into the ballpark and sat in a no-show seat. And, in spite of the tumultuousness of the day, it was most rewarding overall. I did get pictures of four future Hall of Famers—Randy Johnson in the locker room (where cameras aren't allowed), Trevor Hoffman, Sammy Sosa, and Vladimer Guerreo, all in the dugout.

2002 BASEBALL ALL-STAR GAME

In Milwaukee on Monday before Tuesday's game, I crashed both batting practice and the home run derby. I circled the perimeter twice and missed my first chance when one of the guards walked about fifteen feet away to grab a Pepsi that he had stashed. So I kept walking around, and around, and around.

Finally, I found an area where the fans had to go outside the ballpark to smoke. It was surrounded by steel fencing with a male/female hookup. It was completely closed at one end, with about an inch or so between the fence and the stadium. When I walked around to the other end, lo and behold, I found a gap of six to eight inches.

I put my cell phone up to my ear as though I was talking. It wasn't even turned on. And I'm moseying closer and closer. Finally, when nobody is looking, I just zipped right in.

They also had a gala Monday night, and it was absolutely pouring down rain. A friend was supposed to meet me with a ticket, but he didn't come through. So I had to do what I do best—I crashed. I walked up to these two guys at the gate and said, "You know, my wife's with ESPN. She had to leave early because of an assignment. She left her ticket either with you guys or with one of the other ticket-takers here. She's about medium height, dark brown hair . . . "

"Did she have on a white dress?

"Yeah, that's her."

Hall of Famer, Dave Winfield

"Okay, just go right on in."

The next night at the ball game, I sat right behind home plate in a no-show seat, four rows in back of Dave Winfield and his family.

As far as I'm concerned, the tie game was okay. They used all the players, and they didn't have a rule in the book stating what they should do in a case like that. Eleven innings is more than sufficient anyway, so it didn't bother me in the least.

As a crashing event, this was below average—about a C-minus. In fact, there was a party after the game, but I didn't stay for it. I had a plane to catch early the next morning.

WORLD SERIES 1997

The Florida Marlins took the Cleveland Indians in seven games. The illustrious National League party was held at the five star Turnberry Isle Resort and Club just outside Miami on Friday night prior to the first game.

The minute I walked in I spotted a cameraman following this guy by himself with no entourage. I asked the cameraman the name of the gentleman? He replied Mr. Huizenga. That immediately told me he was the Marlins team owner and party host.

I asked, "What's his first name?"

Again he replied, " Mr. Huizenga."

"I know but what's his first name?"

"It's Wayne."

 "Thank you very much."

I told him the only persons I call "Mr." or "sir" are the busboy, the guy who's waiting on me, the man who shines my shoes, the cop who pulls me over—especially a motorcycle cop—the President or Vice President of the United States (provided he's a Republican), and you, if I forget your first name.

Upon approaching Mr. Huizenga near the National League trophy I said, "Hey Wayne, can I get a shot with you and the trophy?"

His reaction was, "Sure, let's hold it."

Great idea.

Owner Wayne Huizenga of the Florida Marlins and the 1997 National League Trophy

A WET WORLD SERIES

When Baltimore won the World Series in 1983, I crashed the club-house as usual after the final game. Eddie Murray, first baseman and future Hall of Famer, was spraying everybody with champagne. He absolutely covered me. I was drenched.

My late-night quote was: "This will be the last time I ever go into the winner's clubhouse after a World Series. I can't stand the cleaning bills!

*Trevor Hoffman and Sammy Sosa in the National League All-Star dugout,
and 'The Cowboy" Gene Autry*

Barry Bonds and Roger Clemens, two future Hall of Famers

Two of the greatest hitters of all time: Tony Gwynn and Reggie Jackson

*Dodger's blue, Tommy Lasorda, and the "Say, Hey, Kid," Willie Mays;
Tommy and I go back over thirty years.*

Mike Piazza in the All-Star dugout and with Johnny Bench

Champions all—Cal Ripken, Jr. and Joe Torre

Earl Weaver and "Perfect Game" David Wells

NBA ALL-STAR GAMES

It was the 1990 NBA All-Star game in Miami. That's when I sat at the press table. There was this little three-foot fence around the court. While everyone was concentrating on the words to the National Anthem on the Diamond Vision, I first put one foot, and then the other, over the fence.

When the National Anthem was completed, some people were sitting down and others were walking to their designated spots at the media table. Every media seat except one was full, and that was for the *Wall Street Journal*. Nobody was there.

The *Wall Street Journal* seat, like all other seats, had an eight by ten sign with their name on it. When I sat down, I took the sign and turned it over (and kept it, as a matter of fact; I still have it). When the *Wall Street Journal* writer finally arrived, he had to find another spot to sit (and I'm sure he was accommodated quite quickly). I was never questioned at all. I just made myself at home, even picking up their phone and letting friends at home know I was at the media table at courtside.

The way I got into the building was through a side door. I just went around trying doors until one opened. It's amazing how lax security was prior to 9/11. Sometimes I could just walk in with the media. Once in, they would go their way and I would go mine. To succeed, you just had to have a little bit of expertise, a lot of luck, good timing, and a great deal of desire.

That reminds me of the way I got in to see the NBA All-Star game in Chicago. It was freezing cold, and a guy opened the door to throw his cigarette butt out. That's all I needed: one cigarette butt out; one Dion flips in.

That same night, my friend Jerry and I walked out of Mike Ditka's club about 2:00 A.M. into a wind chill factor of about 20 degrees below zero! If it weren't for its weather, few people would ever leave Chicago. And in spite of its "chill," Chicago is still one of my favorite cities in the world.

Speaking of crashing All-Star games, I'm also reminded of 1989 when I was with a friend of mine in Houston. He went in the side door. As he went in, the door slammed shut. I couldn't get in. So I walked all the way around to the front, like I belonged, and just walked right in. It was late, and they never gave me a second look.

Jay Leno was the star attraction of the gala party. I crashed and I enjoyed the show in some guy's seat. He turned out to be a friend of mine from San Diego, Patrick Conners. He came in and said, "Dion, you're in my seat." I said, "Hi, Pat, how are ya? I'll find another one." And I did. What do you suppose the odds are on that?

RULES OF THE GAME

There's a hierarchy in gate-crashing, from high school pranks to college diversions, and finally to graduation into the big time of major league baseball, the NBA, the Olympics, Super Bowls, the Kentucky Derby, the Academy Awards, Governor's Balls, Golden Globes, Emmys and too many others to count.

Pat Riley and NBA Commissioner David Stern

DION SAYS:

"I'm not Houdini . . . but I'm close."

As Red Auerbach would say, "That's no cigar."

KEYS TO CRASHING

Never hesitate at the door.

He who hesitates is left outside.

When the guard hesitates, you move in.

Chapter Four

AMERICA'S CUP
1987—PERTH, AUSTRALIA

The Aussies are some of the best hosts in the world.
Their nickname for Americans is "Septic Tank Yanks" because we
allow anyone and everyone into our country.

In 1987, I ventured to Australia for the America's Cup yacht races. Four years earlier, the Australians had captured the Cup from Dennis Conner and the Americans, and we were determined to get it back. I thought this would be a wonderful trip and offer some new experiences. Little did I realize this would become one of my most memorable gate-crashing experiences.

My trip was circuitous, to say the least. I departed the day after Super Bowl XXI on a journey that included stops in Tokyo, Bangkok, Singapore, Jakarta, Bali, Tahiti, plus Sydney, Freemantle, and Perth in Australia. My final, and indeed my most memorable stop, would be the Royal Perth Yacht Club, where the America's Cup land activities were centered.

Crashing was incredibly easy. Upon arrival, I legitimately had need for a men's room. Upon asking for directions, I was pointed "over there." So I went "over there," used the men's room, looked around, and said, "Shoot! I'm in!" I don't know how I got in, but there I was, in! There weren't any guards. Security was extremely lax in those days. It'll be much heavier at the next America's Cup, you can bet on that.

Coca-Cola had a giant hospitality pavilion, and it was about lunchtime. I walked up and asked for the name of the person in charge. Then I went and introduced myself by saying, "Hi, Betty, I'm Dion Rich, Coca-Cola, San Diego."

"Oh, it's so nice meeting you. What are your functions at Coca-Cola?"

"I'm with the PR department."

"Great! Welcome. Come right in. We're having lunch right now. Help yourself."

"Thank you. It's a real pleasure."

I had a couple glasses of beautiful Australian wine and chowed down. I made myself right at home. In fact, I went back each and every day. I even took a ride on the Coca-Cola yacht, got a Coca-Cola shirt, a Cola-Cola beach towel, and a Coca-Cola cap, which I still have hanging among my innumerable artifacts.

My next move was to crash the America's Cup compound. Security was better here, with a lot of personnel standing all around. There were also two guards at the entrance, where there was a line of people with proper credentials. Since I didn't fit into this category, not having credentials of any kind at this point, I came up with an alternative plan. Having noticed the adjacent, low-key shipyards, I decided to breech their more relaxed security.

But it wasn't all that easy, believe me! I managed to get past the gate security all right, but then I had to crawl along a barbed-wire enclosure, down in the water along the rocks, and carefully slide underneath another barbed wire fence so as not to get my clothes torn or wet. I felt as though I was a CIA agent. It was my gate-crashing espionage at its finest.

Once inside the America's Cup compound, I started taking pictures like crazy, including one of me standing on the deck of the winning

Stars & Stripes. Before I knew it, I had used all my film. I realized that I would have to leave the compound in order to pick up more film, I decided I needed a better return plan. I was not exactly looking forward to a repeat of crawling around and under barbed wire, so the adjacent shipyards were immediately out of my plan.

On my way out, I purposely approached a guard, who was engaged in conversation with someone, and made a mental note of the name on his badge. When he stopped talking, I went up and said, "Bob, I have to go get another roll of film for Dennis Conner. I'll be right back. Don't forget me. Remember, I'm wearing the official Coca-Cola shirt." He looked at me and my shirt and acknowledged there would be no problem in my getting back in through his gate.

Mission accomplished! I grabbed a nearby cab, headed downtown to buy a couple more rolls of film, and then came back to the same entrance where Bob was waiting.

"Bob, I'm here with the film."

He waved at me and said, "Okay, come on in."

I then proceeded to take another roll of pictures from which I generated some pretty special photographs, including several of Dennis Conner inside the boatyard and a shot of me walking through a door marked "Team Members Only!"

The next night, the Australian boat, the *Cuckaburra*, threw a big party, and true to my form, I crashed it using my patentable "press credential approach." What I did was go up to the two guards at the entrance and present my phony "ABC-Radio" press credential that says ABC Radio. It has worked for me many times in the past, so I was bullish about my chances this time, even though I was technically in a foreign country. They should have been wise to antics like mine, but I still believed I might be smarter.

In any event, I showed my credential and said, "I'm Dion Rich from ABC Radio in San Diego. They were supposed to leave my event credentials here at the gate." The guard smiled apologetically and said, "I'm sorry, sir. We don't have your credentials, and you can't get in without them."

I asked if he would go up to the central area to see if they have left credentials for me there, knowing all along this is just a stalling maneuver. Then I waited while he went inside this big hanger where they keep all of the sailing gear.

He disappeared for a few minutes and then suddenly reappeared with a big smile, "The head of the party says that any Yankee from San Diego is welcome to come in!"

I walked right in and immediately discovered I was the *only* Yankee at the party. It's nothing but Aussies, and the entire *Cuckaburra* crew is in attendance. The television station had its people there, and there were Australians from all over the country.

It was quite the national event—and one of the year's finest parties.

I partied through most of the night, eating, drinking, and relishing in the fact that I was the only American there. The hosts were extremely cordial, and all of the guests were very friendly, especially when they discovered that I was from San Diego. The only country I've found comparable in friendliness are the New Zealand Kiwis.

(At that time, it was pretty obvious to most that the next America's Cup defense would be in San Diego, so a lot of these people saw me as a good American contact. I, of course, went along with this idea. Later, I discovered through a conversation with a chap from Singapore that at that time, the location for the defense of the America's Cup was very much in doubt, given the favorable wind conditions in Hawaii. San Diego typically has much lighter winds, and some felt this might be a negative factor in choosing the site for the Cup defense. Ultimately, San Diego was chosen, so a good number of the people I partied with that night did come to town four years later to party in my backyard.)

But, back to the pleasures of Perth: There were numerous hospitality suites set up at the adjacent pavilions, and I took full advantage of them during my visit. However, it wasn't quite as easy as I thought it would be. My first ploy was to rely on my phony press card, which I officiously presented to the most gullible-appearing security guard, but to no avail. In all the excitement, I suddenly realized that I again had a very important appointment with Mother Nature, and I immediately took a detour in search of a bathroom.

I'm not inclined to use the nearby public facilities, knowing that each hospitality suite comes equipped with its own well-stocked private bathroom. I started snooping around the complex with the hope that I would find some convenient, unguarded entry point. Spotting a gate without a guard, I quickly walked in and never looked back.

The first suite I crashed just happened to be the Sheraton's where they had prepared a nice spread of drinks and food. After first using their restroom, I was able to relax and enjoy myself to the fullest.

One of the most memorable happenings occurred during the press reception at the press center following the *Stars & Stripes* victory. I crashed two sets of gate security in order to attend. After first sneaking past the security personnel and then penetrating the press reception area, I quietly observed the mechanics of the press conference in progress. A person would state his or her name in front of a microphone, say where they were from, and then ask a question. This process went on for about forty-five minutes before I finally decided to get in on the act.

As a lady with a roving, cordless microphone came within proximity, I tapped her on the shoulder and said, "I'd like to ask Dennis Conner a question."

She turned and asked, "Are you media?"

"Ma'am, I'm Dion Rich of radio station KFSD of San Diego, California, Dennis' hometown."

With a quick "Okay" in my direction, she motioned to the fellow with the other roving mike. He held up three fingers, meaning that I'm the third person in line to ask Dennis Conner a question. Shortly, I'm second in line, and then it was my turn.

"Hi," I said. "I'm Dion Rich of San Diego, and I would like to ask Dennis a question. Will the America's Cup defense be in Hawaii or San Diego?"

Dennis responded, "That's not my decision to make."

End of interview, but I had my fifteen seconds of fame, not only on Australian television, but on worldwide coverage.

A pair of skippers, Dennis and Dion

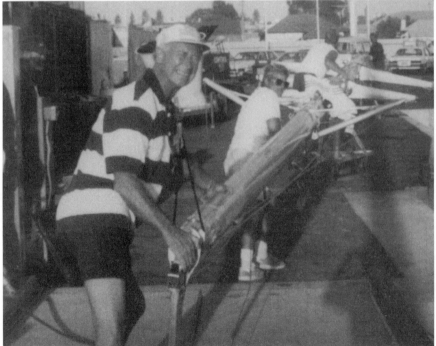

Helping out the crew of "Stars and Stripes"

4651

AUSTRALIA'S DEFENCE AMERICA'S CUP 1987.

AMERICA'S CUP MARQUEE DAY PASS.

Coca Cola

requests the pleasure of the company of

Mr Dion Rich

to our Official America's Cup Marquee No. *2*

Adjacent to the Royal Perth Yacht Club's Fremantle Annexe.

We look forward to your company on *February 4*

for *Lunch* between *0800* and *2000*

Please see reverse for location details

and please present this pass for admission.

This pass does not entitle the holder to parking at the complex nor vehicle entry to the Mews Road area.

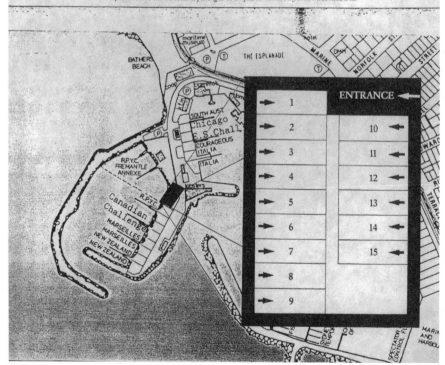

This makes it official

ANOTHER GALAXY FAR, FAR AWAY

The Galaxy at that time was the largest passenger liner to traverse the Panama Canal, and it docked here in San Diego. I heard they were throwing a huge cocktail party onboard for travel agents. I didn't have a ticket, so I did what I had to do—I crashed it.

As luck and timing would have it, I just walk with the crowd onto the gangplank and onto that fabulous ship. The party is adequate, but after checking out the eight massage parlors on board, I know I have to take a trip on this ship. And so I did.

My brother Dan, sister-in-law Sharon, and I flew up to Seattle and took a seven-day cruise to Alaska. This was an excursion that I had to pay for, but the fact that I got a 25 percent discount from my travel agent, made it even more pleasant than anticipated.

RULES OF THE GAME

It's easy to crash an event, but what you want to do is not only crash but attend all the ancillary parties with all the dignitaries. That's what sets the *great* gate-crashers apart.

DION SAYS:

"I'm sorry. I'm just looking for the men's room." *

*Most used quote when I'm stopped by security in the middle of a "crash."

KEYS TO CRASHING

Names, names, names.

Remember names wherever you go.

Keep your name secret for as long as you can.

Chapter Five

HEAVYWEIGHT CHAMPIONSHIP FIGHTS
LARRY HOLMES VS. GERRY COONEY
JUNE 11, 1982—CAESAR'S PALACE, LAS VEGAS
She was a knockout.

Another special gate-crashing moment in my life took place in 1982 at Caesar's Palace in Las Vegas, Nevada. This was the scene of the Heavyweight Championship Fight between defending champion Larry Holmes and challenger Gerry Cooney.

I got this crash off to a good start by obtaining a press pass from a good friend of mine, Chuck Di Rocco, who at that time was the publisher and editor of the *Sports Forum* in Las Vegas. There are two types of press passes for sporting events: One is a working press pass with the best seats in the house; the other is just a pass. This latter pass got me in the door and past the gate, but it didn't entitle me to a seat or to the type of free access throughout the venue that a working pass would have provided.

My initial goal was to secure a decent seat from which to view the fight. Upon entering, I quickly realized there would be more work ahead if I expected to get past the myriad of security guards monitoring the arena and the front row seating area.

When I spotted fight promoter Don King finishing a TV interview, I discreetly sat down beside him, extended my hand, and said, "Don! Nice to see you again!" He meets so many people, he doesn't remember who he has or hasn't met. "Here's my card. I'm Dion Rich, San Diego. Lou Lake, who promoted the Kenny Norton-Ali fight, and I would love to promote a TV fight in conjunction with your syndicate in San Diego," just a little left of the truth.

After taking my card and responding favorably, Don stood up and walked away. There I was, left behind, in the sixth row, ringside, with Jack Nicholson sitting four seats to my left. (This was before I started carrying a camera to document my crashes.)

As I have stated many times before, the primary key to successful gate-crashing is luck and timing. As the main event approached and the seats began filling up, I noticed one fellow who didn't appear to be having luck or good timing. An usher kept bouncing him from seat to seat. He obviously didn't have a ticket either, although he was carrying a camera so it appeared as if he could be affiliated with the press.

My row was now completely full when another fellow moved towards me holding his ticket stub and said, "I think you're sitting in my seat." Knowing that my best defense is a good offense, I extended my hand and said, "Let me see your ticket." I glanced at his ticket, looked at the seat number and said politely, "Oh, sir, I'm very sorry, I am sitting in your seat."

As timing would have it, at the precise moment I was vacating my sixth row seat, the usher was making the kid with the camera move again. This created an opening for me—a seat in the second row. I took it.

Meanwhile, this kid who was being bounced from seat to seat spotted me moving in on his game. He approached and told me I couldn't sit there.

Hello? I looked at him and said, "What do you mean, I can't sit here?"

He started telling me that the usher had just booted him from the seat; but by then I had turned my attention back to the undercard fight and ignored him.

As the seats filled, I found that a movie director was sitting on my left. He, in turn, was sitting next to Ryan O'Neal's son, Redmond. Next to him sat Farrah Fawcett and then Ryan O'Neal. In the aisle-seat on my right was the director's wife, and I was caught between their conversations. Finally, the director leaned over and asked if we could trade seats so he could sit closer to his wife. *Do I mind??!! Let's see, one seat closer to Farrah Fawcett?!!* I gallantly changed seats with him.

We were talking about luck and timing? Not long after, Ryan's slightly obnoxious teenage son, Redmond, wanted to sit next to his dad. So, before you can say "movie star," I found myself sitting *next* to Farrah Fawcett! Now that's what I call perfect timing!

I sat next to her for the entire fight! We even carried on a bit of a conversation, and I have to admit that the fight waned quickly in importance once I was sitting next to her. I tried not to be too obvious looking down the side of her dress, but it was one of the most difficult acts of self-control that I have ever attempted in public. (All she had on was an evening gown and nail polish!) To this day, I am hard pressed to remember details of the fight, even though I had been looking forward to it!

Championship fights have their own regular "name" attendees, and usually there's as much interest being generated around these celebrities as there is around the actual contest and the combatants. Even the larger venues such as Caesar's Palace are relatively intimate when it comes to people watching. In fact, you can sit in the cheap seats and still catch good glimpses of stars that traditionally grace your living room TV.

I also find that most of these well-known personalities, when not the prime target of the media spotlight, are relatively approachable. Most are even agreeable to conversation and consenting to an occasional photo. And once you've had the opportunity to converse with "stars," you realize they're not that much different from any other person you might run into at an event. They are simply fight fans like everyone else.

I happen to love boxing for its simplicity and excitement. Though some would call the sport brutal and barbaric, it possesses a purity and straightforward competitiveness that is rare in many athletic arenas. Championship boxing probably has a much higher concentration of heavy hitters, sports figures, and movie stars than any other media-type event. There is a circus atmosphere that permeates championship fights—especially if you're sitting next to Farrah Fawcett—that's truly center ring.

"The Greatest" Muhammad Ali, and Archie Moore

The lean, mean grilling machine, George Foreman and Evander Holyfield

Sugar and Oscar

PLAYBOY MANSION

In Rick Riley's column in *Sports Illustrated,* he states that I have a picture of me wearing one of Hugh Hefner's bathrobes. I do!

I crashed that particular party at the Playboy Mansion by hopping on the party media bus at UCLA. When it deposited us directly at Hefner's front door, the media immediately started setting up on the front lawn, which is in the shadow of a huge forest.

I, on the other hand, was dismayed to find I needed to immediately locate a bathroom. It was too early to go into the Mansion, where I could have too easily blown my cover and not have been let back in, so I proceeded to hike out into the dense forest—becoming one of the few of Hefner's guests to have helped fight forest fires.

Later, while in the Mansion, I came across a line of about a dozen people.

"Excuse me," I asked, "what's the line for?"

"Hugh Hefner's bathroom."

"Really?"

So for the first time in my life, I got in line to go to the bathroom for the exclusive purpose of sightseeing.

Once inside, my first sight was of a multitude of towels. I swear, he had enough towels to dry off every one of the San Diego Chargers' cheerleaders! And there were four bathrooms just in that one particular area. It might be a whole mansion of bathrooms (and bedrooms) for all I know!

Then I saw his robes in a closet. So I took one, put it on over my clothes, and handed my camera to a man who had just finished washing his hands. "Do you mind?"

"Not at all."

It's a beautiful picture—me in Hugh Hefner's bathrobe.

Hugh and I at the Golden Globes

RULES OF THE GAME

It's an official gate-crash at an event once you are inside without a torn ticket or an official credential, *and* you have established your presence by having your own piece of turf or your own seat, *and* the event has started.

DION SAYS:

"Hugh Hefner and I are on the top of the

NFL hit list—Hefner for exploiting NFL cheerleaders and me for

being on the sidelines during NFL games. You figure."

KEYS TO CRASHING

Treat everybody politely.

Be aware of vacant seats around you.

Be ready for a surprise.

Chapter Six

KENTUCKY DERBY
AND OTHER "HORSE STORIES"
MAY 4, 1996—LOUISVILLE, KENTUCKY
Still looking for respect.

The last time I crashed the Kentucky Derby was when Jerry Bailey won aboard Grindstone in 1996. It was one of my greatest events, as far as publicity is concerned. I was in the picture on the front page of the Lexington paper with Jerry Bailey, along with a complete write-up. The article says I was thrown

Winner's Circle

out. That's incorrect. I have never been thrown out of the winner's circle at the Kentucky Derby, ever.

Crashing the winner's circle is easy. The minute the horses are out of the gate, all 160,000 racing fans are looking at them. All anyone has to do is wait until the horses are going down the backstretch, then step over the short wall and stand still. Nobody even notices you're over the wall. Wait until the race is almost over, then start walking to intercept the winner, the owner, the trainer, and their entourage. They will all be on their way to the winner's circle. It's very easy to tell who the winner is. It's the guy or gal with the biggest smile, the one getting the most pats on the back. Just find him or her and blend in with their group and walk right into the winner's circle for a picture. Then walk right up onto the podium with them for the presentation of the Winner's Cup.

That's what I did. It was the owner, W. T. Young; his daughter; the jockey, Jerry Bailey; the trainer, D. Wayne Lukas; and myself. The five of us up there to receive the Winner's Cup—and to be photographed for the newspaper.

I was in heaven. I was just getting ready to make my inaugural Kentucky Derby speech saying, "Don't you think W.T. did a great job this year?" on worldwide television, knowing all the networks were there, when I felt a tug on my shoulder. I looked around, and a lady said, "Sir, do you have a credential?"

"No, Ma'am, I don't."

"We saw you on television last night."

"Really? How'd I look?"

"You're out of here."

Another official then started yelling, "That's the gate-crasher! Get him out of here!"

No respect! He's supposed to say, "That's the *world's greatest* gate-crasher. Get him out of here." As a further insult, they had a big military sergeant from security come grab me by the arm.

I quickly countered, "That's all right, Sarge. I'll go peacefully."

Then, like at the Academy Awards, they made a rookie mistake. They didn't throw me *all* the way out. They only took me off the podium, which, of course, enabled me to proceed from there to crash the Turf Club, where I got pictures with Connie Stevens and Jerry Hall (Mick Jagger's ex-wife). I missed Stan Musial and George Steinbrenner by five minutes.

(The Turf Club is the big VIP room reserved for members and guests only. In pecking order, the levels begin at the grandstand, rise progressively higher to clubhouse, before peaking at the Turf Club— VIPs only.)

Once again—a little luck and timing!

Jerry Hall, Mick Jagger's ex-wife

Connie Stevens in the turf club, and no relation, jockey Gary Stevens in the Winner's Circle of the Kentucky Derby

Kentucky Derby winner Jerry Bailey at the Belmont, and all-time winner Laffit Pincay in the jockey's room at Del Mar

The Great Willie Shoemaker, and not allowed inside the jockey's room with Mike Smith

---

ROOF OF DEL MAR

Prior to remodeling, there was a back door at the Del Mar Racetrack Reserve Grandstand where an enterprising crasher could enter, traverse up the stairs, and come out onto the roof—the perfect place to catch a few summer rays and have lunch and view the races.

For years, I would go up there during the racing season to work on my suntan and hobnob with celebrities and the media. Finally, the track's PR Director, Eddie Reed, saw me up there once too often and had me removed. This banishment lasted until, unfortunately for Eddie, he died. Needless to say, I immediately ventured upstairs again for more fun in the sun.

During this time, I would also get lunch and take it into a vacant vice president's office where I could eat while overlooking the track and blue Pacific. Then one of the executives, Mick O'Connor, caught me in there and once again it came to an end. But he's no longer with the Del Mar Track, either, so I'm back in again.

Opening Day at Del Mar Racetrack is on Wednesday in mid-July. I now crash it just for old times' sake.

BOOKIE FOR A DAY

It's a Saturday morning, and the Cincinnati Reds are in town for a four-game series with the San Diego Padres. I was having breakfast with Pete Rose, Tommy Helms, and one of the other coaches at the Town and Country Hotel where the team was staying.

Pete leaned over and asked me, "Dion, are you going to the track today?"

"Charlie Hustle"

This being Saturday, the answer was yes. I always go to the track on Opening Day, closing day, the Pacific Classic, Saturdays, and Sundays.

"Oh, yeah, I go up every Saturday."

"Here's fourteen hundred dollars. I want you to put this to win on the only filly in the eighth race. I don't remember her name, but she's the only filly in the feature race."

"Pete, I'm not going to take fourteen hundred dollars up there without you telling me the name of the horse. I've got to know the name of the horse."

"Okay," he said, and off he went to the gift shop to get a daily paper. He came back and said, "Fitzgerald's Place" and gave me the money.

Now I was thinking to myself that anybody could take that fourteen hundred dollars and buy a ticket with it, and if the horse didn't win, you just send the ticket back to Pete. But then I was also saying to myself, *There are twelve horses in the race. If Pete has one, how many horses do I have? I have the other eleven, correct?* It doesn't take a rocket scientist to figure that one out. So I decided to book the race myself.

Fitzgerald's Place went off at about ten to one. It's a mile and a sixteenth. They came out of the gate, and Fitzgerald's Place was in second place going into the clubhouse turn. On the backstretch, she moved into first place. Remembering the odds are ten to one, I was figuring I might end up owing Pete about fourteen thousand dollars. I was thinking that on Monday morning I would have to go to Home Federal and draw out a cashier's check for fourteen thousand dollars.

Now the horses were coming off the final turn and heading down the home stretch. Fitzgerald's Place was about seventy-five yards from the wire. She was still leading, but then she died. She absolutely died. Fitzgerald's Place finished seventh, and I pocketed the fourteen hundred dollars.

And, I'm not kidding, my rear end was sucking wind right there at the finish.

RULES OF THE GAME

A crash is a failure if it doesn't culminate with exposure on television, in a newspaper, or in some other publication covering the event. This documentation is important to prove that the crash was successful. It's easy to say that you crashed a major event, only to have someone doubt your word. I have become so good at getting television and newspaper exposure that it is an event when I don't make media coverage.

DION SAYS:

"If I were a betting man, I would bet on myself every time."

KEYS TO CRASHING

Take immediate advantage of an opening.

Once committed, keep moving.

Keep all options open.

Chapter Seven

WINTER OLYMPICS
SARAJEVO – LILLEHAMMER – ALBERTVILLE
"The Boss" gives up his gloves.

SARAJEVO

Another of my all-time gate-crashes took place overseas. The year was 1984. The place, Sarajevo, Yugoslavia. The event, the Winter Olympics. Communist security forces were everywhere, and because of the terrorist attacks at the 1972 Munich Olympics, I expected crashing would be especially tough. It is one thing to operate outside the friendly and well-understood confines of the U.S., but in Sarajevo I would also have to be wary of a hostile government and an equally wary security force, most of whom spoke little or no English.

Due to some lengthy airline delays and bad connections, I arrived in Sarajevo in late evening the day before the opening ceremonies. To make matters worse, I had no tickets to any of the events. I was going to have to crash every venue. But, as usual, I was up to the task, so crash is exactly what I did.

Transportation to and from all skiing and alpine events was by bus, but bus tickets conveniently included an entry ticket to the event. The first day, I did buy a bus ticket, but I also made the acquaintance of a local Yugoslavian fellow who just happened to be a security guard. Even better, we hit it off.

Once we arrived at the ski slopes, he would escort me around and actually facilitate my crashing. Together, we walked right across the ski slope and into some of the compounds. I had no credentials, but by acting like I was a member of the press and belonged, I got in without any problem.

Every venue provided a unique security challenge, but getting into the ice skating event turned out to be relatively easy. I simply approached the guard at the entrance gate, showed him my phony AP credential, and told him I was looking for the photographer with Associated Press. He told me he wasn't supposed to let me in, but he let me go in anyway. I told him I'd be right back, which was the farthest thing from the truth.

This turned out to be one of the most impressive events I attended, with the Soviets taking first and second places and a British couple taking third. It was also great because three San Diego friends actually saw me on television. Being seen at a Super Bowl is an accomplishment, but being seen at the Olympics is extraordinary. At a Super Bowl, you can actually figure out when TV cameras are going to be pointed in your direction. Figuring this out at the Winter Olympics is much more difficult.

While the security remained intimidating, many of my more typical gate-crashing approaches worked quite well. Once in, I tried to make myself immediately scarce. This is extremely difficult when every seat is taken and there is standing room only. At the ice skating event, I happened to be standing without a seat when the same security guard who had let me in came by and asked if I had found my friend. Without missing a beat, I nodded "yes" while pointing across the way to my fictitious "friend." Fortunately, he smiled and walked away, but my heart took a few beats that didn't seem natural.

The Olympic Press Center was impressive, and large enough to house reporters from all over the world. My plan for entry was simple and worked beautifully. All I did was to patiently watch the crowd of reporters and newspeople going in and out for the right opportunity and then timed my entry to coincide with a large flow of traffic.

In general, security guards are positioned on either side of an entering crowd. As people stream in between them, they are often too busy watching the outer edges to see anyone slipping through in the middle. I count on this in many of my crashes, and this is exactly the approach I used for entry into the press center. The only added problem lay in the fact that I had to get through not one but *two* security checkpoints, so I had to time each with perfection. Fortunately for me, it turned out that communist guards are no different from their counterparts all over the rest of the world, because it worked to perfection. Patience is a real virtue in any type of crashing.

I also slipped into the secured compound following the women's downhill skiing event. This was the year that Americans Debbie Armstrong and Kristin Cooper went one, two, gold and silver. With no idea of how well she would perform, I had obtained Debbie's autograph prior to her race for friends back home. At that time I still had not started carrying a camera. She would actually come home with the gold medal, which made my crash that much more special.

All in all, the Olympics in Sarajevo were a very special experience for me. I met some wonderful people along the way, including locals, media from the U.S., and athletes from all around the world. The only problem I found lay in the distance and traveling time between events, so I wasn't able to attend a few of my favorites—like hockey and the ski jumping. Sometimes you can't be everywhere you want to be, and the Winter Games are that kind of venue.

LILLEHAMMER

Lillehammer was the biggest and best of all. High on my list of highlights was crashing figure skating—always the hottest ticket at the Winter Games.

I entered this venue by going in with the crowd. This was before 9/11, so the entrance was manned by volunteers—again, two people, one on each side, taking tickets, no turnstiles. I walked right in between the two of them, with the crowd. They weren't looking for crashers. (Since 9/11, they do a complete body search, and they *are* looking for for terrorists as well as gate-crashers.)

With Lady Luck prevailing, I sat next to Billy Kidd, the first-ever American to win an Olympic medal in the alpine events. I not only got a picture of him, but also one with Scott Hamilton, former skating gold medalist. He was broadcasting for CBS-TV at that time.

Members of the U.S. Olympic Bobsled team

I also crashed the pressroom. My first attempt—through the front door—failed. They stopped me walking in. I then went around checking doors. None would open. There was also a guard standing at the back door, but by then I *really* wanted in. So I just walked past him as though I owned the place.

The minute I was in, I got my picture taken with two members of the U.S. bobsled team. Then I took advantage of the opportunity to ask for a media credential chain. Not having a credential to hang on it, I wore the chain only. With my ski jacket zipped up part way, no one could tell anyway, and I looked like I belonged.

Now comes the best story of Lillehammer. I left the Winter Olympics on a Saturday night and get a hotel room in Oslo. On Sunday, I was supposed to leave on a Delta flight to New York City. But before I left, I treated myself to a going away brunch at the fancy, four star Plaza Hotel.

As I got up to leave, I saw two buses outside with CBS signs in their windows. I took out my press credential chain and hung it around my neck, zipping up my jacket to hide the missing press credential. I looked very official and, it being very cold, just like everyone else boarding the buses.

Seeing a guy charting on a clipboard, I went up to him and said, "Excuse me, sir. Are those buses going to the airport?"

"Sure. Are you with CBS?"

"Yeah, I'm with CBS, L.A."

"Oh, Okay."

Look him straight in the eye. Don't smile. Don't laugh.

"CBS, L.A. First bus is full. Get on the second."

I went to the second bus. The bus door was open. I got on.

Crashing a media bus is as easy as anything. It's a slam-dunk. You just hop on. If you can't crash a media bus, you shouldn't be in the business.

So, I was on the bus. I went all the way to the back for two reasons: one, I didn't want anyone to see me, and, two, the bus door was still open and it was *really* cold. I pulled my collar up, but I made sure my credential chain was still showing.

I always carry a *USA Today* so that if I have to wait for anything, I have something to do. I pulled it out and started reading. The bus filled up. The door closed. The bus was off.

When we got about ten minutes outside Oslo, I knew they were not going to throw me off the bus, into the snow, so I started exchanging Olympic pins. These pins are made up by whatever TV network does the games, by the advertisers, the sponsors, and the sports federations. Some of them are really quite beautiful and valuable, and I've been collecting them since the 1984 Calgary Olympics.

Anyway, I was thinking maybe some of the CBS guys would be on my Delta flight from Oslo to New York City, so I asked, "What flight are you guys on?"

"Oh, we're on a charter."

Uh-oh! Boy oh boy, the bells started ringing. Charter, charter, charter . . . Charters do not come up to Delta's gate. It doesn't take a rocket scientist to figure that one out. Right away I realized I had hitched a ride on the *wrong* bus.

"Well, are you going to Oslo International, aren't you?"

"Oh, no, no, no. We're going to a small airport on the outskirts of town."

"Really?"

We were heading towards Sweden. I had a 1:00 flight to catch. I was looking at my watch. Only a miracle was going to save me from missing that plane. I went up to the head guy on the bus with his clipboard.

"Excuse me, sir. I got on the wrong bus."

"You *are* with CBS?"

"Yes, Dion Rich."

He spoke into his phone, "Do you have a record of a Dion Rich?"

The crackly response was, "No."

"Evidently, he got on the wrong bus."

With that, they pulled off to the side of the road into a little circle where the snow was ass-deep. We were *way* out in the middle of farm country on a Sunday. No telephones around. I stepped down from the bus.

You think I didn't have good luck? As I was stepping down, an empty cab pulled up at the same exact moment. I started yelling at the cab. He couldn't hear me. The bus driver started honking. I got my bags off the bus, waved goodbye to CBS, and caught the cab. It was a $35 cab ride. Luck and timing.

At the Oslo airport, along with the intense security, there were hundreds of people lined up trying to catch flights. I had no choice but to crash the line in order to make my flight to New York. The line was formed like an elbow at a 90-degree angle. I placed myself near the front, put my bags underneath the velvet rope, and walked away for five minutes as if I was going to make a phone call. When I came back, I slipped under the velvet rope, picked up my bags, and commented to no one in particular, out loud, "Boy, I still couldn't get through to L.A."

No one knew I crashed the line, so no one cared. And I'm glad I did. No sooner did I get on that plane than it took off.

ALBERTVILLE

For the Albertville Winter Olympics, I remember leaving the hotel early in the afternoon the day of the opening ceremonies. I left without gloves, hat, or topcoat because it was comparatively warm and the sun was out.

I hung out with a couple of friends that I'd run into, and, before I realized it, the sun was down and it was time to go to the opening ceremonies. It was too late to go back for my gloves, my hat, and my topcoat.

I was able to crash the opening ceremonies by going in with a crowd, but it took two tries to succeed. At the first gate, an official asked me for my ticket. I told him I was looking to buy a ticket. He said, "You have to go that way."

I went in another gate. I waited until there was a larger crowd, and this time I made it. As had worked for me many times before, I just walked right in between the two men taking tickets and sat down in a no-show seat on the third row from the bottom.

There was a plastic parka tucked onto the side of each seat, and as time went on, it was getting colder and colder. And I was getting colder and colder. Finally, I grabbed the plastic jackets from the adjacent seats and put them on. Then I took a third one for good measure and stuck it inside my belt.

About two-thirds of the way through the opening ceremonies, I decided I *had* to get closer to a heater. I was just getting too cold. I got up and walked around to the top of the stairs where I ran into Pat O'Brien who was working the Olympics for CBS.

I found I was standing behind the American TV compound, and I still had both of these parkas on. One of the female contestants turned around and said, "That's the way to stay warm."

I said, "Boy, is it ever! I ran off without my gloves, without my hat, and without my topcoat. I'm freezing to death."

A man next to her turned around and said, "Here, take my gloves."

You'd have to be purple and in a prone position before I'd give you my gloves—and that's if I *knew* you. I responded with an enthusiastic "Thank you, sir!" and put on the gloves.

I walked up to where CBS had a couple of big spot bulbs off to the side for light. They were maybe 500-watt bulbs. I backed up to them like they were a fireplace, and I finally thawed out.

Once I was 100 percent warm, I started thinking, "I have to give this guy back his gloves." I went back, took out one of my business cards, and said, "Sir, here's my card. If you ever get to San Diego, look me up for anything you might want. Your gloves made my day. By the way, what's your name?"

"George. George Steinbrenner."

And it was.

Artist Peter Max, Luge medal winner at Nagano

Olympic Gold Medalists Bruce Jenner and Carl Lewis

RULES OF THE GAME

You never have home field advantage.

DION SAYS:

"If you're bold and adventurous, you're going to get thrown out.

Your luck won't last forever.

People say, 'Dion, if you think you're so smart,

why do you get thrown out of so many places?'

I say that in order to attain greatness in life, one has to be willing to

take chances. And that's exactly what I do."

KEYS TO CRASHING

Look the part.

Play the part.

Be the part.

Chapter Eight

2002 WINTER OLYMPICS
FEBRUARY 6–FEBRUARY 17
SALT LAKE CITY MEDAL LEADERS

GERMANY	35
UNITED STATES	34
NORWAY	24

Surrounded by the Secret Service

It all started on Valentine's Day, Thursday, February 14, 2002. That's when the Secret Service arrived at my home in San Diego, knocked on my door, and announced—after first showing their identification—they wanted to talk with me. Talk to me they did, for about half an hour, including reading aloud a document essentially stating that if I crashed the Winter Olympics in Salt Lake City—like I had in the past and like I did at the Super Bowls—it was going to be a federal offense.

Needless to say, I bought a ticket at every event I attended and made *sure* it was torn, because I didn't want *any* difficulty with the Secret Service. I thought that would end it, but they weren't taking any chances. From the time I got off the plane in Salt Lake City until the time I got back on the plane to go home, a four-person, Secret Service team tailed me the entire time. They never let me out of their sight.

I did take a picture of them, though, but only of their backs. Even so, my heart really started pumping. It never pumps when I'm crashing something. I'm always cool and collected. It's like water running off a

Your Secret Service at work in Salt Lake City

duck's back, because it's just so easy for me. But not with this picture. I just knew that at any moment they were going to turn around and catch me in the act. Another problem was my camera. If you don't hold the shutter button down and count two seconds while holding the camera perfectly still, the picture will be a complete blur. For the first time, two seconds seemed an eternity.

I stayed at a private house in Salt Lake City, and there was always a Secret Service SUV (one of the three—maroon, dark blue, and tan) outside the house. No one from the team cracked a smile or waved the entire time—that is, until I got on that Delta flight back to San Diego.

One day I stopped in to see a buddy of mine named Vinnie who happened to be in the ticket business. When I came back the next day, he said, "Dion, the Secret Service came in asking about you." The next day, a female reporter at one of the venues told me, "Dion, the Secret Service came up and were asking about you." Even so, I didn't know they were actually trailing me continuously until my friend Hal, who was giving me a lift in his car, said, "Uh-oh. We're being followed." He pulled a quick u-turn right in the middle of a double-double, and the Secret Service also pulled a quick u-turn right in the middle of the same double-double.

I knew then they were being *really* thorough, so I might just as well get with the program. Not long after, I was going home one night, when the cab driver said, "Uh-oh. You better get in that house right away because we're being followed." I said, "Not a problem. I couldn't be in better hands. Four badges and four guns. It's the Secret Service, and I've never been so safe in my entire life!"

Unfortunately, they did scare me off. I didn't crash anything. End of an era for me. In fact, it got so if I didn't see them I'd get nervous and call the hotline number of the Secret Service. I got on a first-name basis with Mike. I'd call in and say, "Hey, Mike. This is Dion. I'm at 4th and Elm, or wherever. I don't see the guys." I was just as nervous without them as with them. A lot of people count sheep if they can't sleep. Well, I count SUVs.

The first venue I went to was figure skating. I had no sooner walked in than a Salt Lake City cop comes up and says, "Mr. Rich, excuse me, but my supervisor would like to have a word with you."

His supervisor was Sergeant Steve Cheever of the Salt Lake City Police Department. After introducing himself, Sergeant Cheever got right to it. "Mr. Rich, we don't want to embarrass you, but we would like to talk with you; please step over here."

I said, "Oh, Sarge, just call me Dion. I'm on a first-name basis with the LAPD, the San Diego PD, Miami PD, Atlanta PD, and now the Salt Lake City PD. Just call me Dion. I don't have to be called Mr. Rich."

"Fine," he said. "We'd like to show you where you can go and where you can't go. Step over here. Now, see that door marked 'NO ACCESS'? You can't go there. See this door over here? It's marked 'NO ACCESS,' too. You can't go there. See your ticket? You are restricted to that area and that area only."

"Can't I get up to go to the bathroom?"

"Yeah, you can do that if you want."

I'm restricted. The Secret Service is following me, and now the Salt Lake City Police are following me.

Official business over, the sergeant relaxes and says, "Geez. You're quite the celebrity, aren't ya?"

"Did you read Rick Reiley's column in *Sports Illustrated?*"

"I haven't, but everybody else has."

"Well, I just happen to have an extra copy." I pull out the article and extend it to him.

"Will you sign it?"

"Sure." I autograph it "To Sergeant Cheever. Best Wishes, Dion."

"Can we get a picture with you?"

They already had a picture of me at the entrance captioned, *"If you see this man, don't arrest him until he gets inside, then arrest him and call the proper authorities."* Now they want a group shot?

"Sure," I said. "Can we use my camera?" We took a great group shot, which I had made into an eight by ten for them.

The article in *Sports Illustrated* and all the publicity about me started when a reporter by the name of Les Carpenter at the *Seattle Times* called me the Monday prior to the Super Bowl to write an article on me. It was because of that article that Rick Riley wrote his column in *Sports Illustrated.* And it was because of Rick Riley that I became even more notorious than I had been previously. Probably fifty radio stations all the way from Canada to New Zealand called for interviews, and ESPN, CNN, and other networks were after me. One guy in Canada asked me, "Mr. Rich, at your age of seventy-two, when are you going to quit this?" I told him, "I'm too young to quit." Another guy from Canada asked, "Do you feel that you're doing your country a service or disservice?" I said, "Sir, I'm merely pointing out that the security in my country sucks."

Billy Kidd, and Dion with the Salt Lake City police and an Olympic executive

RULES OF THE GAME

The challenges you face will give you the opportunity
to test and hone your skills.

DION SAYS:

"Don't mess with the Secret Service."

KEYS TO CRASHING

Never lose sight of your goal.

Stay loose.

Get lost in the crowd.

Chapter Nine

TWO TOUGHEST CRASHES
PLANET HOLLYWOOD &
SUPER BOWL XXXIII, DENVER'S VICTORY PARTY
Sometimes it's ego; you just have to be there.

The easiest crashes, by far, were Super Bowl I and the Battleship *New Jersey,* but the toughest crash of my life was when Planet Hollywood opened in my hometown of San Diego. I got thrown out twice before I finally made it in on the third try.

I was not sent an invitation. For me not to obtain an invitation for something in San Diego is rare. When I mentioned this to my friend Jeff, he said, "No problem. I'll get you in if you'll get me into the Academy Awards." (The Academy Awards were two weeks later.)

Planet Hollywood was as important to me as the Academy Awards since I had already crashed them before on many occasions, so I said, "You've got a deal."

"Okay. Here's what we'll do. I'm going to meet you at the Westgate Hotel. You're going to have to be the date of a friend of mine in order to get in."

"That's okay. Once we get in, she goes her way, I go mine."

The week before the grand opening, Junior Seau of the San Diego Chargers football team had a party at Planet Hollywood. I did not have to crash. I knew people who had invitations and attended as their guest. While inside, I cased the joint.

You always want to case a joint. If you can, it's best to check out a place a week or less in advance to see how you can get in, what doors are going to open, if you will have to go through the kitchen, if you will have to go through a side door, what side doors open, what side doors don't, what access you have to the kitchen or elevators. As a rule, fire exits open only from the inside by a push bar, which makes them of no use going in.

Anyway, I was checking out Planet Hollywood, and I found a front porch segment with a door near the men's room that lead to a balcony near the front. I was thinking this could offer an excellent possibility of getting in. Then I made a rookie mistake.

On a door in front of me was a sign that read "EMPLOYEES ONLY." Usually, an employees-only sign doesn't bother me at all, so I went in this door, found out the manager's name, and went to talk with him. Turns out he was the guy who handled all of Planet Hollywood's new openings. He was the advance man. Once one Planet Hollywood is open, he moved on to the next restaurant scheduled to open.

So I told this manager, "I'd like to work a trade with you on the opening next week."

"What are you doing back here? No, No, No. I don't have any use for any trade. You're not supposed to be back here!"

Oops! So now he knew who I was. BAD news!

The next week it was time for the San Diego opening. This Planet Hollywood opening turned out to be probably the biggest, with the highest amount of hoopla, of any restaurant in San Diego that I know of. They had bleachers. They had red carpet. They had media, radio and television, promoting and giving away bleacher tickets. Of course, I wanted no part of the bleachers. (In fact, I'd be ashamed if somebody caught me in the bleachers at any function like that. I want to be *in*—being a part of—*not* watching.)

So I was at the Westgate Hotel waiting for my friend as prearranged. Right on time, a Volkswagen pulled up with Jeff and his girlfriend in the back seat. The girl driving was my date—the one I was supposed to go in with.

Once out of the car at Planet Hollywood, Jeff gave me a name to use at the front desk. Only trouble was, it didn't work. The name was not on the register. Even worse, at the same moment I as being rejected, the manager I had talked to (behind the employees-only door) walked up, recognized me, and said, "I told you last week you weren't going to get in here."

I quickly turned and made like I was walking out. Once I saw him go back into the restaurant, I doubled back, this time making my way *past* the people at the desk. Fortunately, there were only a few people on desk duty, and they were all busy with other guests.

Just when I was thinking I'd made it, out comes the manager again. He spotted me and said, "You're *still* out here!" This time he got two yellow-coat security men. They marched me arm-in-arm out onto the street.

Determined to get back in, I walked around to 4th Avenue, all the while mumbling to myself. I just can't believe the trouble I'm having, while *all* the celebrities of San Diego, the Mayor, the City Council members, the Supervisors, dignitaries, and *all* the people I mingle with are *all* in there. There *had* to be another way in, and I was going to find it!

Suddenly, luck was on my side again. Just when I needed him, a street sweeper appears holding up a small radio-station-distributed, Planet Hollywood credential. He says to the crowd, "Who wants this?"

I quickly responded, "I'll take it. What do you have to have?"

"Give me twenty bucks."

"I'll give you ten."

I knew he'd take the $10 because nobody else would have the guts to go in on a pass like that.

As soon as it was in my possession, I rushed home, put it on the neck chain I got from the pressroom in Lillehammer, and was off again—looking quite official with the credential around my neck.

And it was worth it. The opening was big—the biggest I've ever been to in San Diego. As I walked around, with one eye open for the manager and the other searching out celebrities, I ate, drank, talked with friends, took some pictures, and had a great time.

And I didn't run into the manager again, not even once, until I was leaving at the end of a full, satisfying evening. I waved to him and said, "Nice party, pal."

I credit this as a double-crash, (1) because I had to work so hard to get in, and (2) because of the look on that manager's face at the party's end. He was clearly thinking, *What?!! Him again? I threw him out TWICE!*

Sharing Planet Hollywood tough crash with TV news anchor Paul Bloom

CRASHING BY TELEPHONE

Not long after I crashed the Planet Hollywood opening in San Diego, I got a long distance phone call from a young lady in Nashville, Tennessee, who has read the front page Kentucky Derby article about me published in the Louisville newspaper. She has gotten my phone number from information (I'm listed).

She asked if I could teach her how to crash the Planet Hollywood opening in Nashville. I told her I had been thrown out of the San Diego opening twice before I finally made it in, but that I would give her my best advice.

The first thing I told her was to go in and case the joint a day or two before the opening and find out where the doors—back doors, side doors, all doors—were located. She should also check out the kitchen with its entrances and exits.

I also told her she might want to go in an hour to an hour and a half before they opened up, then head immediately to the ladies' room. If there were two commodes, she could sit on one of them with the door locked and read a newspaper until the opening was in progress. As long as there were two commodes, she should be home free. I never heard from her again so I took it for granted she made it.

SUPER BOWL XXXIII

The second toughest crash of my "career" was when the Denver Broncos beat the Atlanta Falcons in Miami in the Super Bowl XXXIII. I had all kinds of problems getting into the Denver victory party that night.

The party, which is always held at the hotel of the winning team, wasn't scheduled to start until about three hours after the end of the game. This was to give the players time for interviews and then to get dressed up and get to the party.

Parking at the hotel was going to be a major problem, but I thought I had it licked. Due to surgery following a severe skiing accident in Bulgaria after the Sarajevo Winter Olympics, I had acquired a handicap placard that I carried with me when I travelled. So when I drove up to the hotel parking lot for the party, I held up my handicap sticker as though I wanted handicap parking.

"Sorry, sir. Unless you're registered at the hotel or have a bonafide credential for the party, you can't get in."

I drove away, waited a half hour, then pulled up to the parking lot attendant again. This time I said, "I have to pick up a wheelchair patient."

Now this usually works. You'd be surprised. A parking lot can be full. The handicap lot can be full. Deliver this line while looking the attendee straight in the eye, and a parking place of some kind can usually be found.

Not this time. The attendant said, "I told you, you can't get in unless you're registered at the hotel or you have a credential for the party."

I turned around again, but by then it was raining. They get a lot of rain in Miami. Two blocks away, I pulled into a church parking lot that was totally empty. As I was walking back to the hotel in the rain, I saw a couple of kids in their early twenties scaling a barbwire fence.

I'm in my seventies and in good shape, but without the help of these kids, I never would have gotten in. They literally pushed me over the barbwire fence. I cut up my hand pretty good, but I got in. Once over the fence, the kids went one way, and I went another— through the employee's entrance and straight to the party.

The first thing I discovered upon arriving was that the party was in two parts—a front part for cocktails, which was in full progress, and an inside part for dinner, which was yet to come. They weren't letting people inside for dinner yet, so I walked down a couple of doors and entered the dining room an alternate way. The waiters, bartenders, and a supervisor with a clipboard were all just standing around, so I stood around too, doing my utmost not to look conspicuous. Fortunately, they let me be.

Finally, the guests started coming in, and I got a glass of wine from the bar and started mingling with the players. And what made the cuts on my hands and all worthwhile was getting a picture with John Elway, Shannon Sharpe, and Terrell Davis!

It turned out to be one great party!!

RULES OF THE GAME

If you're thrown out, it just means you have another chance to succeed.

DION SAYS:

"My avocation doesn't pay much, but it's a lot of fun."

KEYS TO CRASHING

Case the joint.

Always have another way in.

Patience is your middle name.

Chapter Ten

SUPER BOWL I
JANUARY 15, 1967 – LOS ANGELES COLISEUM
*Thank God it wasn't the Gatorade era or Dion would
have gotten soaked.*

Super Bowl I—better known as "that American Football
League–National Football League First World Championship Game"
(the longest title in history)—was the game where the Green Bay
Packers beat the Kansas City Chiefs thirty-seven to ten in the Los Angeles
Coliseum. Super Bowls weren't actually referred to as Super Bowls until
Super Bowl III.

This was one of my easiest crashes of all times. I practically knew
the whole Kansas City Chiefs team, as many of them came to my Bar
of Music during the old AFL days. Even Kansas City Head Coach Hank
Stram came in one time, sat down, and had a Coca-Cola. After notic-
ing how many of his players were there, however, he didn't even
finish his Coke and walked back out. Lots of sports writers came in
also, including Jack Murphy and Jim Murray. It was a hangout for both
media and players alike.

For Super Bowl I, the Kansas City Chiefs stayed at a hotel in Seal
Beach, which is a coastal town just south of Los Angeles. I arrived early
on a very foggy, miserable Sunday morning and followed their busses
up to the Coliseum. It was like being in a parade, complete with a big
police escort. I stayed right on their tail through the fog and through the
red lights until we got to within about two miles of the Coliseum. Then
I sped ahead, parked my car, and waited at the players' entrance.

The moment the busses pulled up, I walked in with them, right into the locker room. Then, after borrowing one of the coach's jackets, I went down the tunnel and onto the field, right on the sidelines. I stayed there on the field the entire game. Back in those days, they hardly checked you.

After Kansas City got beat thirty-seven to ten, their post-game locker room was a complete morgue. This is the way it is whenever a team loses, no matter what the sport. I got out of there in a hurry and went over to the Green Bay locker room. Nobody stopped me. I just walked in like I owned the joint.

Attitude plays a part in getting in. Attitude, luck, and timing, and feeling like you belong. Also, you don't look the guy at the door in the eye. There's no eye contact. And you walk through at a special pace—not slow and not fast, but with a deliberate, *almost* fast pace, as though you have to be in there at that particular time.

As soon as I entered the Green Bay locker room, there on the TV platform was NFL Commissioner Pete Rozelle with Bart Starr and Coach Vince Lombardi. Pat Sumerall of CBS was interviewing them.

Super Bowl I, first world championship trophy, with Vince Lombardi and Pete Rozelle

I decided that would be a good spot for me, so I got up on the podium with them—just in time to get included in a photograph taken by the late Dan Tichonchuk, photographer for the *San Diego Union-Tribune.* When I showed the picture to my friends, they all knew Bart Starr and Vince Lombardi, but they didn't know the other guy—Pete Rozelle—who later became the greatest Sports Commissioner of all time.

I just did it for the thrill. I wanted to be close to the action.

I remember there was no victory party after the game. In fact, that first year, the Commissioner's party (later to become one of the hottest tickets in sports) was a Friday afternoon cocktail party on the mezzanine floor of the downtown Sheraton Hotel. Hors d'oeuvres and cocktails. I crashed it, but it wasn't worth the effort.

RULES OF THE GAME

Analyze your successful crashes. Experience is your best teacher.

DION SAYS:

"It took me longer to get to an inside telephone

than it did for me to get inside."

KEYS TO CRASHING

Attitude

Luck

Timing

.

Chapter Eleven

MORE SUPER BOWLS
MIAMI, NEW ORLEANS, LOS ANGELES, HOUSTON, PASADENA, AND STANFORD

People have said that at one Super Bowl Dion even went on the field with a pail of water during a time out. Dion neither confirms nor denies this accusation.

SUPER BOWL V

Super Bowl V took place at the Orange Bowl in Miami and pitted the Baltimore Colts coached by Don McCafferty against the Dallas Cowboys and Tom Landry. Baltimore won the game sixteen to thirteen on Jim O'Brien's last second, thirty-two-yard field goal.

As time was ticking away, I was able to get right next to Coach McCafferty, and all of the television cameras are trained on us. It was some of the best prime time coverage I ever received. I actually gave the coach a friendly pat on the shoulder as we walked off the field— a gesture, seen on television, that didn't escape the attention of my friends back home in San Diego.

There was a huge post-game party in Hollywood, Florida that featured the winning Baltimore Colts. It was held at a big resort hotel, and again security was almost non-existent. I was able to pull Johnny Unitas aside and collect several autographs for different friends. They also had a gourmet, sit-down dinner that I attended without invitation, sitting next to NBC, Hall of Fame sportscaster, Curt Gowdy.

The Golden Arm, Johnny Unitas

After a while, I decided to go visit the Dallas post-game party, where I learned a valuable post-Super Bowl lesson. If you are going to go to both teams' parties, always visit the loser's party first.

The Dallas party was like a morgue. There was hardly anyone left. Losers go home early, while winners party all night. If you're going to be a party crasher, make sure you attend them in the proper order. This way you will never be disappointed.

SUPER BOWL VI

NFL security had gotten wind of my sideline and locker room act by now and wanted to put a quick end to it. They were especially annoyed with all of the newspaper and television publicity I was getting. They were determined to thwart my efforts, which only fueled my gate-crashing fire that much more.

In Super Bowl VI, Dallas beat Miami convincingly twenty-four to three, and I defeated NFL security five to nothing. In fact, I pulled off a Super Bowl double hat trick. First I remained on the sidelines during the entire game at Tulane Stadium in New Orleans. Second, when the game ended, I was standing next to the winning coach, Tom Landry. Third, I made it into the Cowboy locker room and stood on the podium with Dallas running back, Duane Thomas, during the trophy presentation and his short interview with CBS' Tom Brookshire and Jim Brown.

For the second half of the double hat trick, I absconded with Tom Landry's "coaching hat." It had "Landry" painted on the sweatband, and it fit comfortably in the pocket of my overcoat. I'm not a thief, but the opportunity was just too good to pass up.

In addition to my double hat trick at Super Bowl VI, I also scored an additional prize. I was able to crash the Cowboy's victory party by ducking underneath the flap in the tent, where I immediately spotted this gorgeous young lady—a twenty-one year-old co-ed at the University of Texas in Austin. We danced the night away. Besides being a lovely young lady, she just happened to be Tom Landry's daughter.

SUPER BOWL VII

The occasion was Pete Rozelle's annual Friday night extravaganza, which was being held aboard the Queen Mary in the Long Beach harbor prior to the Los Angeles Coliseum's second Super Bowl. This was by far one of the sporting world's most elegant and exotic parties, put on expressly for the owners and their guests.

About 11:00 P.M. that evening, I was savoring the aire of hierarchy, wondering what the land-bound commoners were doing, when there was a tap on my shoulder. I immediately turn around and gaze up at a 6-foot, 5-inch, 230-pound giant with a glare in his eyes that signify he isn't on a mercy mission.

This was Jim Kensil, who at that time was the top official for Pete Rozelle. He continued his offensive by jabbing his forefinger virtually to my nose and asking, "Is your name Dion Rich?" I looked him in the eye, blinked, and said, "Yessss . . . " With forefinger still menacingly in my face he said, "If we catch you on the field Sunday, we're throwing your ass out of the Coliseum. Do you understand?" Figuring it is no time to rock the boat, I blinked, gulped, and dutifully nodded.

Two weeks later in *Newsweek*, there is a perfect shot of winning coach Don Shula and me on the field at the end of the game. Miami defeated Washington fourteen to seven, to complete the only undefeated season in NFL history.

SUPER BOWL VIII

On January 13, 1974, Super Bowl VIII took place at Rice Stadium in Houston. This was the first and last time a Super Bowl had been played in the State of Texas. It was Miami against Minnesota. This contest had a personal significance for me, as the NFL was really starting to crack down on my crashing.

On the Friday night before the game, NFL Commissioner Pete Rozelle threw his annual pre-game party. After walking through the front entrance like I owned the joint, I stood off by the side to observe how they were taking invitations.

My rookie mistake was to be standing alone, which made me a much easier target to spot. As "unluck" would have it, the head of NFL Security, Frank Dunahay, saw me from a short distance away. He immediately came up and said, "Hello, Dion. Do you have an invitation?" When I replied that I didn't, he responded with the predictable, "If you don't have an invitation, you must leave." Unfortunately, he had a front and side view photo of me, so I didn't have a good excuse or an escape vehicle.

I had violated one of my cardinal rules of gate-crashing, namely, to always mix with the crowd and never stand out alone at an event I am crashing. Even armed with the photographs, the security staff would have had a much harder time finding me if I had made it inside and was mingling amongst the 3000-plus attendees.

The worst part was that I had planned on having a gourmet meal on the NFL. I knew my attempt at gaining this prize had been soundly thwarted. Not wanting to further antagonize security, I quickly and quietly left, found a nearby restaurant, and had a nice, second-best, Texas-style rib dinner. Because this time the tab was on me.

SUPER BOWL XIV

By 1980, some six Super Bowls later, I had become *persona non grata,* not only on the field, on the bench, in the press box, in the locker room, at cocktail parties, and at Rozelle's party, but virtually at all events sanctioned by the NFL.

At about 9:00 P.M. the night of Super Bowl XIV's unparalleled Friday night bash, Jerry Mancus, producer of the musical "Hair," and I are walking up the steps of the Pasadena Civic Auditorium to join in these fine festivities. All of a sudden, we hear a male voice booming at the top of his lungs, "There he is! Grab him! Get him! Don't let him get in! Take his invitation!"

This vocal-chord-bursting voice belonged to none other than Jim Kensil, performing his official security duties. It had taken the NFL seven years to learn my true identity, and another seven years to finally stop me from crashing one of their affairs. From Kensil's standpoint, I had just made his day.

An incident of this nature would perhaps embarrass or impede a "normal" person. Not being normal or embarrassed, I knew my work was cut out for me and took on the challenge.

Inside, another close friend, Ray Malavasi, the head coach of the Los Angeles Rams, was asking Jerry what happened to me. And Jerry was explaining that although Kensil has confiscated my invitation at the door, he was expecting me to join them in about five minutes.

Well, Jerry was wrong. After I nonchalantly surrendered my ticket to purposely throw the NFL off my track—knowing I didn't need their invitation to crash—it took me closer to ten minutes. But I got in, passing as a waiter. It turned out to be the only NFL party I ever got thrown out of *before* I got in.

As far as the game is concerned, the Pittsburgh Steelers came from behind to defeat the Los Angeles Rams thirty-one to nineteen.

SUPER BOWL XIX

Super Bowl XIX was held at Stanford Stadium in Palo Alto, California on Sunday, January 20, 1985. In that game, the San Francisco 49er's defeated the Miami Dolphins thirty-eight to sixteen.

This was a memorable Super Bowl game for me because of two factors:

First, it was very cold, with the game-time temperature hovering in the forties and a wind-chill factor even lower. I had on a pair of long underwear, two pairs of socks, and an extra sweater, and I was still nearly freezing my posterior off.

The second major significance to this game was the high degree of security around the stadium and on the field. The NFL had brought in both the Palo Alto Police and the Sheriff's department. Then, for added security, they brought in police dogs. Because the NFL thought they weren't doing enough in keeping people such as myself off the field, they brought in "rent-a-cops." It was almost unfair. I even considered changing my cologne to throw the dogs off the scent.

As usual, I came to this game very well prepared. I was equipped with a disguise and a walkie-talkie to appear more like a bonafide event operative. Both my disguise—mustache, cap, and thick bifocals—and my walkie-talkie were necessary in keeping up with the increasingly elaborate security measures that the NFL was throwing at me. The walkie-talkie didn't even function and it was small, but perfect for my application.

I was selective in choosing my entry and noticed a young rent-a-cop standing at an entry to the field. I just walked right past him as I chatted away to nobody on my walkie-talkie. It worked like a charm. I walked right onto the field, where I enjoyed every minute of the game.

Tom Flores, Dick Vermiell at Super Bowl XV, and John Madden, Super Bowl XI

Broadway Joe Namath, and Miami Coach Don Shula

Theismann rhymes with Heisman, and Bob Gibson with Deacon Jones

Jim Brown and Walter Payton

RULES OF THE GAME

Always go to the loser's party first.

THE NFL QUOTE:

"Rich is not a big deal, except that afterward he will call the press and tell them what he has done. He's just an aggravation."

— Jim Steeg, NFL Executive

DION SAYS:

"The crasher in the new millennium will have to be very high-tech oriented. New gadgetry and electronic security will make a typical crash a lot more difficult and time consuming."

KEYS TO CRASHING

Remain anonymous

Never stand alone

Pick your spots

Chapter Twelve

SUPER BOWL XXIII
JANUARY 22, 1989 – JOE ROBBIE STADIUM, MIAMI
SAN FRANCISCO 20 – CINCINNATI 16
Dion's Waterloo

For more years than I can count, I have been penetrating a varied and often elaborate NFL security net. Even as their security people became more and more determined to thwart my gate-crashing antics, I could always come up with yet another creative approach for getting onto the field. By Super Bowl XXIII, I had used phony credentials, disguises, fake walkie-talkies, and other creative means in evading capture. Having succeeded for almost three decades, I figured they would catch up with me sooner or later, but my bet was on later. I did not realize to what great new lengths they were willing to go to stop me.

Super Bowl XXIII was to be my "Waterloo" —where the NFL put into action their *own* clandestine "sting" operation. As the game approached, however, I was feeling my usual confidence. I had been up against the NFL security team many times before, and each time I had come away victorious. The official record was Dion: twenty-one to NFL: zero (I had only missed one game, Super Bowl III, due to a long-planned skiing trip).

Thus I approached this Super Bowl like I approach all important gate-crashes—with supreme confidence. My plan had actually come from a good friend of mine, Rodd Sidney. He proposed we obtain a couple of game tickets from his handicapped brother, enter the stadium in wheelchairs, and sit in the special handicapped section in the stadium. We carefully strategized our entrance, and I was feeling quite secure about getting us both into the stadium. Plus, I would be bringing a phony credential as backup.

On the Tuesday of the week of the Super Bowl XXII, I got a phone call from a Charles Noble, of *Sports Illustrated.* He wanted to do a story on me and my Super Bowl exploits. Naturally I was very flattered.

The following day, I got another call, this time from a John Kincaid. He said he was with a South Florida trade magazine, and he also wanted to do a story on me. Suddenly, I was quite awash in the glow of my popularity. It turned out that it was an NFL string operation.

I said, sure, I would be happy to do an interview, figuring it would add yet another entertaining episode to my repertoire. When he asked me how he could contact me in Miami, I felt no hesitation in giving him the number at the condo in Ft. Lauderdale where I would be staying. He closed by alerting me that a writer by the name of Felix Eads would be doing the story on me, and that Felix would be contacting me.

So I was feeling great when my friend Rodd and I got on the plane for Miami that Wednesday. What I didn't know was that John Kincaid, whom I believed to be a South Florida trade magazine person, was actually a private eye in the employ of the NFL. I also didn't know that John's cronies would begin tracking my every moment the minute I stepped off the plane.

The pre-Super Bowl parties were just getting into gear when we arrived, and I had particular interest in attending Pete Roselle's annual extravaganza. A couple of my friends went early, but I knew if I got caught, they'd throw me out. So I waited. At about 10 P.M., I was able to slip in the back door with no problem and make up for lost time. And considering the NFL sank more than half a million into the party that year, there was still time to enjoy the festivities.

Saturday night Rodd and I crashed the NFL Properties party, an event sponsored by the corporation that has the rights to all concessions for the Super Bowl—hats, t-shirts, jackets, and memorabilia. Then on Super Bowl Sunday, it was party time once more, this time at a pre-game party at the Hilton Hotel. Only problem was, Rodd lost his keys to the rental car—the car with our wheelchairs locked inside. Without wheelchairs, our handicapped tickets are useless.

So we spent an hour getting a lift back to the airport to fetch another set of keys. We finally arrived back at the party, late. Our arrival time though was perfect. A couple of guests with entry stickers attached to their lapels were just leaving, and they happily gave us their stickers. Thus, after building up a splendid appetite, we embarked on one of my very favorite pastimes—complimentary buffet lines.

After the party, it was time for the main event. Armed with wheelchairs and our handicapped tickets, we arrived at Joe Robbie Stadium. It was packed, and there were a lot more people looking for tickets than selling them. I was a little tired but was looking to finally meeting Felix Eads, the writer who was to do a story about me. We'd made arrangements to meet in the wheelchair section.

At that point, I still had absolutely no idea the NFL had undercover people on me my entire stay. They had been to parties with us, at the hotel, and even into the handicapped parking lot. Yet, despite their surveillance, they were giving us free reign to pretty much go wherever we wanted.

We had no trouble crashing the main gate or the press area gate. We rolled right past security people, and not one of them even asked for our credentials. From there we entered the stadium underneath the tunnel, then took turns wheeling each other around the field perimeter and taking pictures as we went. Eventually we caught the elevator to the wheelchair section.

We remained in the wheelchair section the entire game. Super Bowl XXII turned out to be the only time I have ever sat through an entire playing of the Star Spangled Banner. By game's end, I was having some funny vibes, but we still wheeled down to the area where the presentation of the Lombardi trophy was taking place.

Suddenly, a fellow walked up and said, "Hello, Dion. I'm Sergeant Palmer of the Miami Police Department. You are out of here!"

We didn't have a chance with three undercover Miami cops glued to our tails. As we are poised to make it so, Sergeant Palmer announced that the NFL wanted to have a word with us. This scared the daylights out of me. In my wallet was a phony NFL security card, which if found could possibly cause them take me into custody.

They didn't search us, so for a moment I thought we were out of danger. A few minutes later, however, another fellow walked up and said, "Hi, Dion. I'm Felix Eads, Private Investigator—the one who's supposed to do the story on you for the South Florida trade magazine." After a pause for effect, he added, "Dion, you've got to stop this crashing. You're costing the NFL thousands of dollars each year to try to keep track of you, and it just can't go on any longer. You are going to have to stop. This has to be your last."

After Felix finished venting on us, we found out there was another NFL official who wanted to have a word with us. After making us wait for thirty to forty minutes, Ed Dubois finally arrived to begin reading us the riot act. And if we weren't already scared enough about what the NFL might do to us, he informed us they can charge us with trespassing.

The lecture finally ended with Ed warning us to also stay away from the post-Super Bowl party tents, where there would be pictures of us should we decide to crash. He then told us to scram.

We took off as fast as we could go and straight for . . . you guessed it—the gigantic NFL after-Super Bowl party! Because I needed a short pre-party refresher nap, my buddy Rodd arrived at the party ahead of me. No sooner did he make his entry than he ran right into Ed Dubois—the same Ed Dubois who has just kicked us out of the Super Bowl. Ed turned to Rodd and said, "Boy, you sure made a quick recovery. Where's Dion?" Rodd told him that I was so scared after the lecture that I have hastily beat a retreat to Ft. Lauderdale.

In truth, I had taken a quick nap in the car. Upon waking, I headed straight for the NFL party, where, fortunately, none of the security people saw me. I partied with friends for a while and left—in time to crash the San 49er's victory party.

The following day, I telephoned *Sports Illustrated* writer Charles Noble to give him the complete story of the NFL's sting operation. He was so interested in the details that he called the NFL to see if he could obtain photographs from them. He couldn't, but he did write a story that made a great conclusion to a very enjoyable portion of my NFL gate-crashing career. Upon post-game reflection, I came to the realization that the twilight was upon me when it came to activities that were making the NFL see red—those activities being crashing the field, locker room and press box. If I didn't soon choose voluntary retirement, the NFL would make it involuntary.

They called a truce. The NFL leaves me alone in my territory; I stay out of theirs. The NFL isn't at all concerned with my pre-game or post-game activities. They aren't even all that concerned with my game day movements as long *as they don't include trips to the playing field, locker room, awards ceremony, or press box.*

On the plus side, I'm still able to crash all the parties I want, and I plan to continue partying forever.

RULES OF THE GAME

Always be careful. You may be your own weakest link.

DION SAYS:

"I have always lived for the challenge,

and it has served as my motivation

to overcome obstacles and penetrate barriers

that other men only dream about."

KEYS TO CRASHING

Don't rush

Think like a security guard

Go for it

Chapter Thirteen

FOOTNOTES TO GREATNESS

"I hope I never grow up."

— Dion Rich

Each of my all-time favorite gate-crashes has a special flavor. The Super Bowls were inarguably the toughest events to crash and, because the NFL had my number from Super Bowl VII on, offered the most exciting, minute-by-minute drama. On the other hand, the Olympics, while relatively easy to crash, are world arenas incomparable to any other sporting or media events.

The wild card element of crashing in a foreign country, where the repercussions of an unsuccessful crash can be far more serious than in the U.S., can be very exhilarating. There is also the aspect of testing good old American creativity and resolve against a foreign system and culture that gives my trips overseas a particularly challenging and interesting edge.

Highlights would also have to include the Heavyweight Boxing Championships which, as events, are truly unique in and of themselves. They represent a microcosm of society where you see more important and influential people in one small area than in almost anywhere else you go in the world.

Mayor Rudy Guiliani, and Governor Pete Wilson with his wife Gayle

As my reminiscences draw to a close, I want to welcome those of you who believe they have enough passion and ingenuity to enter the world of gate-crashing. As you are aware by now, it is an avocation that I personally really enjoy, but I do want to caution you about a few things.

- Gate-crashing is not for everyone. If the challenge of it doesn't excite your senses, start your brain cells working, and bring gladness to your heart for being alive, I recommend you stick with buying tickets or watching from the comfort of your couch.

- The more you know about your venue and the surrounding security, the more likely your success will be. This knowledge is imperative in the collective work ethic you must display.

- You must approach your crashes cost-effectively. Don't create an unnecessarily steep downside. Although I have not always followed my own advice and have gotten stranded in some pretty destitute places, take heed and watch your expenditures closely. A good crash is one where you get a lot of benefit for very little out-of-pocket expense.

- If you do decide to fly to Florida for a Super Bowl and expect to crash every event, remember hotel rooms, plane tickets, and rental cars cost money. Party crashes are important in this equation as they typically bring food, drink, and entertainment for the price of a free admission.

- You have to be a good gate-crashing consumer. Everyone will be looking for ways to separate you from your money, so always be on your guard for salesmen, swindlers, and con artists.

- Pickpockets deserve a paragraph of warning of their own. Pickpockets are a special problem, especially when traveling overseas. Keep a money belt and fasten it securely to your ankle,

President Gerald Ford, Ollie North and Donald T. Sterling, owner of the Los Angeles Clippers

waist, or chest. There is no faster way to ruin a trip than to get pickpocketed the first day. (I know—I was pickpocketed within a matter of hours after arriving in Havana in 1996; what I was doing in Havana when Americans were banned from travel in Cuba is a whole other story).

- Develop a worldwide network of friends. They are mighty handy in a tight spot. I have friends in a few countries around the world, and I still keep in touch with them.

- A good memory helps, and practice can make it better. Remembering names and faces will help you greatly when traveling and crashing.

- When approaching crashing as a part-time hobby, try to develop a career path that coincides with or supports your crashing endeavors. My choice was owning and operating a cocktail lounge with entertainment, which I not only enjoyed but it provided me with a steady stream of new contacts. I also happen to love sports, so a sports bar was a good fit. If your thrill is rock concerts, get a job as a security guard to provide a legitimate reason to be on the ground floor. You also have the added advantage of getting paid to spectate. From there, you can learn the ropes and entries of each forum and devise ways to penetrate security networks.

You don't have to become a Secret Service or FBI agent to learn the tricks of their trade. Just learn to think *like* a security guard when devising plans for stealth. Unfortunately, or fortunately, you'll find quite a few rent-a-cops and security people come from the Social Security retirement lines or are teenagers just out of high school with little or no expertise in guarding gates.

- You are not the only concern of those in charge of security. They have schedules, deadlines, and duties to fulfill. If you can remain on the scene long enough, sometimes they simply lose interest in you. This allows for easy entry some of the time and often ends up taking very little effort on your part.

- If you're stopped and asked for your identification in a long line, take your time finding your license or press card. A few guards will grow impatient and either let you in or just simply forget about you. This technique of stalling has worked wonderfully for me at Super Bowl parties. At any busy function, people get distracted very easily and thus create numerous opportunities for you to crash.

- The stalling tactic also works well if you are ever apprehended by a rent-a-cop. You can simply start spinning a long tale on how you got lost or confused, or were looking for the telephone, the men's room, or left your camera inside, or "My wife has the car keys."

- If you are caught in the act, one of the easiest methods of getting off the hook is to simply admit your mistake, apologize and look for a new entry way.

- Everyone in a position of authority has an ego. By acknowledging their position and authority, you are complimenting them. When you make them look good, they will usually go easier on you. And, by all means, *don't* make them look bad in front of their superiors!

- Never lose sight of your payoff when crashing. Keep your goals in mind. Everyone has different ideas of success. For me, some of life's greatest pleasures are quite simple. I love a fine meal, good conversation, and the attention of a beautiful woman. What are yours?

- Knowing your motivation is vital in developing your skills over a long period of time. Don't forget, I have been at this for more than fifty years, and crashing the Super Bowl parties of 2003 gave me as much enjoyment and satisfaction as did midget auto races at Balboa Stadium in San Diego in the mid '40s .

- Believe in yourself. Successful gate penetration does wonders for self-confidence. Success, in turn, breeds more success, and it won't take you long to feel good about your abilities.

- Success and self-confidence in gate-crashing easily transfer to other aspects of your life, career, and relationships, and even to your overall competitiveness and success in athletics. You will find yourself more willing to take a gamble and less concerned about the eventual outcome.

- Losing simply means you have another chance at winning if you are willing to try again.

- Crashing helps you deal with adversity in life by putting you in the driver's seat. You *can* control your own destiny.

- The media might try to make you believe otherwise, and your friends may laugh at your antics, but don't ever let them dissuade you from your mission. Many of these people are simply afraid to take charge in putting excitement in their lives. They are also the ones who will sit and complain in front of TV reruns, while you are out creating your own feature-length films.

THE MOST IMPORTANT SKILLS IN CRASHING:

1. **Timing.** You have to know when to make your move. For most of us, this skill comes with experience, though some people seem to have an innate sixth sense for slipping in at *exactly* the right time. Timing is also based upon observation—picking out the pitfalls and dangers associated with the venue you are attempting to invade, as well as picking your spots. But without proper timing, your plans can easily go astray. You need to know when it's time to start, time to go, time to leave, and time to abort your crashing.

   Timing is important in almost every significant aspect of life.

2. **Luck**. There is a lot of luck in good timing, making it another essential element in a good gate-crasher's repertoire.

   Luck is truly an innate quality. You either have it or you don't. Good timing is often a byproduct of being lucky. If you have luck on your side, you will find your crashing experience to be generally enjoyable and successful.

   Most people know if they are lucky or not. How do you make out when a difficult situation comes your way? Do you usually end up on top? While there are some things you can do to enhance your likelihood of being lucky, you will discover quite readily if you possess the luck of a good crasher.

3. **Knowledge** is another important gate-crasher prerequisite. You develop knowledge through contacts and experience. If you already know the layout of the venue you are going to crash and the names of the front door ticket takers, you have a big advantage on the guy who just flew into town with no contacts, the wrong clothes, and bad breath. He might be successful in spite of himself, but it's certainly not the way to bet.

After crashing multiple Super Bowls and other events, I developed quite an arsenal of tricks and was almost always able to find the right combination of surprises, disguises, and contacts to weasel my way onto a playing field, locker room, trophy presentation, or press box. This knowledge also came into play in crashing events such as the Summer and Winter Olympics and the America's Cup. The same basic techniques can be used over and over again in different places. The events and people may change, but tactics are usually quite similar.

4. **Courage.** In successful gate-crashing, you have to have a multitude of intestinal fortitude—better known as "guts"—to take risks. Every second you are operating in a clandestine fashion, you are in jeopardy of being discovered and tossed out of a particular event, or even being put in jail.

    You have to be able to handle periodic stress and to switch gears in a moment's notice. You have to be able to stand up to that security guard looking you right in the face and convince him or her that you have a legitimate reason to be there.

    You also have to have the guts to admit you are in the wrong when you are caught in the act of illegal entry. Hopefully, this is not something that will happen to you very often, but you have to be prepared because it *will* happen.

5. **Attitude.** Lastly, if there is truly one idea I want to impart to you from all of my gate-crashing, it is to *live life with a youthful view.* This isn't to mean that you should be childish, but rather *live life in a constant state of wonder.*

    If we slow our pace down once in awhile, we can see the beauty of life all around us. Though our bodies age, we can still maintain some degree of childlike innocence in our human interactions.

When people ask me, "Dion, when are you going to grow up?" my rebuttal is, "I hope I never grow up. I want my obituary to read 'Cause of death: *Living!*'"

I have met young people who appear to be very old because they never move outside their very small circle of friends; and I have met aged senior citizens who are as spontaneous and outgoing as any four-year-old child. So, who is really old: the young people with old minds and youthful bodies or the old people with young minds and worn-out bodies?

Occasionally, a reporter or friend will ask me what I want out of life. My answer is typically, "More of the same." I am happiest when I'm among friends or crashing a big event. Sipping a complimentary glass of champagne and munching on a delicious variety of seafood hors d'oeuvres is my definition of bliss. This is not a difficult reality to create if you put your mind to it.

I hope I can continue my lifestyle for another twenty years. As long as the mind keeps functioning and the body is willing, you can keep looking for me in trade publications and on television from time to time.

You won't be seeing me on the sidelines of any upcoming Super Bowl games or in the locker rooms, but if you visit the post-game parties, I'll be found mingling amid the celebrities somewhere between the bar and the buffet.

I'm extending an open invitation to anyone out there who enjoys living life a bit on the edge and is motivated by risk and excitement to enter into the wonderful world of "gate-crashing."

And if by chance you should find yourself some Sunday afternoon on the sidelines of a professional football game and a security guard should approach you and ask for your field pass, just tell him that Dion sent you!

RULES OF THE GAME

To attain greatness, you must be willing to take chances.

DION SAYS:

"The security landscape has changed.

It's really tough these days after 9/11."

KEYS TO CRASHING

When caught admit your error and gracefully leave.

Timing is just as essential when leaving as when arriving.

Exit smiling.

A Tiger and a King

Stevie Wonder and Arnold Schwarzenegger

Lunch with Linda Evans and 1952 chauffeur of Hollywood star June Haver at the Mother Goose parade

Hulk Hogan and Elton John

TV's Jenny Jones and Mr. Las Vegas Wayne Newton

In the pits at Long Beach Grand Prix, and with Miss Budweiser owner, Bernie Little

Jane Powell and aerobic queen Denise Austin

"There goes the greatest hitter in the world" Ted Williams, and "There goes the greatest receiver in the world" Jerry Rice

The great Johnny Longden and Dion with the mayor of Philadelphia Ed Rendell

1988 U.S. Men's and Women's Olympic Volleyball Teams

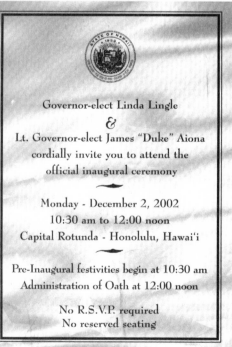

Governor-elect Linda Lingle

&

Lt. Governor-elect James "Duke" Aiona
cordially invite you to attend the
official inaugural ceremony

Monday - December 2, 2002
10:30 am to 12:00 noon
Capital Rotunda - Honolulu, Hawai'i

Pre-Inaugural festivities begin at 10:30 am
Administration of Oath at 12:00 noon

No R.S.V.P. required
No reserved seating

Governor Linda Lingle of Hawaii at her Pre-Inaugural festivities

Chapter Fourteen

A FINAL FAREWELL
SUPER BOWL XXXVII
JANUARY 26, 2003 – SAN DIEGO, CA

"All good things must come to an end."

— Dion Rich

The week before Super Bowl XXXVII, two special agents—one from the Criminal Intelligence Unit of the San Diego P.D. and the other from the Department of Justice—come out to my home. The first thing they want is a picture of me in their official capacities. The second thing they want is to have their picture taken with me in a totally unofficial capacity. I am happy to accommodate both requests. In parting, they request that I call them when I have purchased my Super Bowl ticket so they can come over and take a photograph of it.

I did buy Super Bowl tickets. I bought two for $1,750 and sold them to friends for $2,000. Then I took the $2,000 and bought two more. After selling one to another of my friends for $2,000, I now had one remaining ticket—for myself—for free *and* I also got to sit with them. Can't beat a deal like that.

When the special agents came back out to my house to photograph my ticket, they informed me they would be my chauffeur to and from the game on Super Bowl Sunday. When I told them I had some TV and radio interviews lined up, they were actually very nice and quite accommodating. We arranged for them to pick me up at 12:00 noon.

They showed up at my house at 11:45, ready to go. As I got into their undercover SUV and headed for Qualcomm Stadium, I was reminded of the Secret Service-driven SUVs that followed me at the Winter Olympics in Salt Lake City. Just when I was trying to decide whether it was nicer to be "escorted" in one than "followed" by one, we arrived at a parking lot adjacent to the stadium entrance.

Walking from the parking lot toward the metal detectors (like the ones at airports), one of the agents called over a sergeant in uniform. We now formed a mini-parade—the sergeant was in lead position, then me, with the two special agents in plain clothes bringing up the rear— moving toward the metal detectors. When we reached the gate, one of the game's security supervisors reached out to me and said "Hi, Dion. How are you?" After shaking my hand, he pulled me over and said, "You're not getting in here."

Just like in a movie, one of the plainclothes' agents flashed his badge and said, "San Diego Police Department." With that, we all went in, and I actually hung out with them for a couple of hours before the game. They were also quite accommodating with my TV interviews. When the time came to take my seat, the agents knew exactly where it was, and they kept an eye out that I *remained* sitting in it. The only crashing I did that day was two friends' sky boxes.

After the game, I was expecting a lift home. Although the special agents walked me in, they got a call about a disturbance in the "Gaslamp" district and had to leave without me. So I called my girlfriend and met her at the McDonald's across from the stadium for a ride home.

I found out later that every cop, every security guard, and every employee had a picture of me. A friend of mine at the SDPD secured this copy for me. I also understand that the FBI circulated their own picture of me. It's possible that my days of crashing Super Bowl games are over. The good news is that there are still a lot of other fields left to be conquered.

CALIFORNIA DEPARTMENT OF MOTOR VEHICLES IMAGE
DION D RICH

V0611098	**EXPIRES:** 11/20/2007 **CLASS:** F	**SEX:** M
HAIR: BRN	**EYES:** BRN **HEIGHT:** 600	**WEIGHT:** 180

DATE OF BIRTH: 11/20/1929
ADDRESS: 3920 LELAND ST F18, SAN DIEGO, CA 92106
PHOTO DATE: 11/08/2002 **PHOTO OFFICE:** 506 **APPLICATION DATE:** 11/08/2002 **APPLICATION OFFICE:** 506
ISSUE DATE: N/A **ISSUE OFFICE:** N/ **RESTRICTIONS:**

SIGNATURE:

Dion Rich

FINGERPRINT:

Photo circulated at Super Bowl XXXVII

Gate-crasher's Super task (appeared on the front page of the *Sacramento Bee*)
By Matthew Barrow
SACRAMENTO BEE STAFF WRITER

San Diego—At the age of 73, Dion Rich has a shock of white hair and a pair of twinkly eyes that make him look like someone's cuddly grandpa.

Don't let the appearance fool you.

The San Diego resident is a crafty devil, as sly as a fox, a man of many faces. The "World's Greatest Gate-Crasher."

If there's a prestigious invitation-only event in America, Rich has sneaked into it.

But he's really made a name for himself by sneaking into the most exclusive party there is: the Super Bowl. Rich has failed to infiltrate only one Super Bowl—No. III—and it was only because he was on a skiing vacation at the time.

"You have to have ice water in your veins, that's for sure," Rich said.

But Rich facing security measures designed to handle greater threats than him, admits his streak may end Sunday in his hometown. With about 3,000 law-enforcement officials on hand, Qualcomm Stadium will be as tight as an Army base Sunday. Military jets will enforce a seven-mile no-fly zone around the stadium, and Coast Guard rescue helicopters have been making practice runs to the stadium in the event something goes wrong. The FBI and the California National Guard will be there as well.

Most of the parking lot around the stadium already is fenced off, limiting access to only a few spots. Anyone who enters must pass through one of 90 metal detectors manned by dozens of yellow-coated security guards. Everything from coolers to binocular cases are banned, and the few small items that are allowed will have to go through a screening process similar to the one used at airports.

Big Brother will be there, too.

Rich's biggest obstacle likely will be a $400,000 camera system that allows authorities to look into every nook and cranny in and around the stadium.

The system is unique in two ways.

First are the 50 cameras themselves, which swivel from high atop the stadium and zoom in with capabilities that rival the stuff of spy thrillers.

"They can read the program in the hand of a fan or the license plate on a car," said Al Tumini, president of San Diego-based eVideo, the company that developed the technology. And while traditional camera systems can only be viewed from a central control room, the digitized images Sunday can be see from just about anywhere.

Officers on patrol will be able to look through portable computers. And using the correct passwords, law-enforcement officials in downtown San Diego and beyond can log onto the Internet and watch live shots.

"The FBI in Washington could look in if they wanted to." Tumini said.

In the past, officers would have to radio back and forth to the control center to get assistance. With the camera system, that lag time is eliminated.

"If officers respond to a situation, we'll be able to know if they need backup before they do," said San Diego police spokesman Dave Cohen. "We'll be able to see a larger portion of the area than them."

The police tested the system Dec. 8 when, appropriately the Raiders and their famously rowdy fans visited the Chargers. Police that day arrested 69 people, threw 33 drunken revelers into detox and cited 38 others with misdemeanors. The cameras also helped nab a fan who had been tossed out and was trying to sneak back in.

If past Super Bowls are any indication; there will be more of the same on Sunday.

Two years ago at Super Bowl XXXV in Tampa Bay, two Massachusetts men arrived at the gate in surgical scrubs insisting they were paramedics assigned to work the game. They were turned away and caught later while trying to sneak in. Another man was accused of trying to buy a jacket from a security guard. A third man was arrested when he tried to sell an undercover officer a bogus Super Bowl volunteer T-shirt and credential.

New Orleans police reported far fewer attempts at last year's game, mainly due to what was then the largest, (tighest, and—at $7 million)—the most expensive security setup for a Super Bowl.

Yet, somehow, Dion Rich still sneaked in and did so in six minutes, according to several journalists who witnessed his covert entry.

"A guy from Canada once asked me if he thought I was doing a service or a disservice to my country," Rich said. "I said, 'Sir, I'm merely pointing out that the security in my country sucks.'"

Still, Rich admits that this will be his toughest mission to date. Not only does he have to thwart the camera technology, but in his hometown, the police know exactly what he looks like.

"We're definitely aware of him," Cohen said. "It'll be a challenge for him this year."

So Rich has decided to warm up for the big event.

On Friday morning, reporters were milling around the Media Center, waiting for Raiders coach Bill Callahan to show up for his 9:30 press conference. One of them—a tall fellow with a head full of white hair and twinkly eyes—didn't belong to any media organization and had no credentials.

No one knew how he had gotten in or whether he had also been present at Buccaneers coach Jim Gruden's press conference an hour earlier.

The World's Greatest Gate-Crasher had struck again.

KNOW HIM FROM ADAM
DION RICH
BY ADAM SCHEFTER/DENVER POST SPORTS WRITER

Dion Rich is the man the NFL knows, but wishes it didn't. He has sneaked into the past 33 Super Bowls, not to mention a multitude of World Series games, title fights, America's Cup races, Kentucky Derbies, Olympic events and even the Academy Awards. After posing with Gwyneth Paltrow, the Academy of Motion Picture Arts and Sciences mailed Rich, far right, an official letter of complaint that characterized him as "a particularly persistent trespasser." How insulting, he thought. He prefers to think of himself as the World's Greatest Gate-crasher.

Adam Schefter: How do you do it?

Dion Rich: Believe me, everyone asks me that question. In order to crash a Super Bowl, it takes a little luck, a little skill, lots of desire, lots of hard work, connections and lots of (expletive deleted). Now, if there is such a thing as reincarnation, if I don't come back a fireplug, I'll undoubtedly come back as a burglar.

AS: Why do you do it?

DR: It's the thrill of it, getting my adrenaline up. Actually, I had fantasized all my life over working for the FBI, the CIA, and the Secret Service. Any clandestine operation has intrigued me. But for the Winter Olympics, I didn't have to join the Secret Service. They joined me. They followed me the entire time, from the time I got off the plane until the time I got back on it.

AS: Are you planning to crash this Super Bowl?

DR: Absolutely. I have to. It's in my backyard. What do you

mean am I crashing this Super Bowl? Silly question. Now remember, I'm planning. I never boast that I'm going to crash anything.

AS: Does it give you extra pride to be able to try to pull this off in your hometown of San Diego?

DR: I thought 9/11 was bad with New Orleans. That was a piece of cake. This is going to be tough. If I pull this one off, I just might be the world's greatest gate-crasher. In fact, people ask me, "Do you really feel that you're the world's greatest gate-crasher?" And I always say: "I've detested braggarts all my life. For me to tell you I'm the world's greatest Gate-crasher, I really feel would be bragging." But I can unequivocally say, "I'm one of the greatest who ever lived."

AS: Do you feel that Osama bin Laden could have done the same thing you did?

DR: You know, it's quite possible, but highly inconceivable, because bin Laden does not possess my expertise.

AS: If you possess so much expertise, why have you gotten caught?

DR: In order to attain greatness in life, one has to be willing to take chances. That goes with any aspect of life.

AS: Hardest entry you've had?

DR: Head and shoulders above all of them: Planet Hollywood in my own backyard in San Diego. If I can't get an invitation through my connections, it's pretty tough. Sure, I could have sat up in the bleachers with the people that got freebies from the radio stations, right? I'd be embarrassed if any of my people would see me up in the bleachers.

AS: Do you get fired up on Super Bowl Sunday?

DR: Really fired up, with butterflies in my stomach. But Super Bowl VII, when the Dolphins beat the Redskins 14–7 in the L.A. Coliseum, is when they found out my true identity. They found out because I'm so obvious. I'm right where the action is. I can't stay behind the scenes and still be doing it. But I wouldn't have pictures with Tom Landry and Vince Lombardi and all the rest of them.

AS: What does it feel like to be carrying Tom Landry off the field after he won a Super Bowl, as you did"
DR: Actually now that I know I'm in the Pro Football Hall of Fame in that same picture, it feels pretty good.

AS: Do you plan on carrying Buccaneers coach Jon Gruden or Raiders coach Bill Callahan off the field this year?
DR: Negative. I will never, ever step foot on the field, in the locker room or the press box ever again. I gave the NFL my word in Super Bowl XXIII. That's when they put a sting oper-ation on me. From then on, they give me my territory and I gave them theirs. I stay off those three points of interest to them, and I can crash all the parties I want. In fact, I'll crash a party and some of the owners will be in a group, and I'll see one of them look at me, then the other look at me, and they'll say, "That's him, that's the guy right there."

AS: Who is the coolest person you every met?
DR: Joe Namath, head and shoulders above all of them. He's the most down-to-earth guy you'd ever want to meet. George Foreman is another one. Wayne Newton is another. He puts his arm around you, shakes hands and says thank you. Like with Lauren Bacall, I put my arm around he, she yelled, "Take your hands off me!"

AS: Is Lauren Bacall the coldest person you've met?
DR: No, because she at least allowed a picture. Barbra

Streisand is. And Barry Bonds. I'm at the All-Star Game in Texas. I see Barry Bonds, I ask him for a picture and he says, "No." So I go up to this guy and say, "Excuse me, sir, I'd like to get a picture with Barry Bonds, but I don't want to interrupt him, so I'll wink at you when I want you to take the picture." I get behind Barry Bonds, I wink, and now it looks like he's posing with me. But just because a person won't take a picture with me, I don't have any resentment. In order to dislike a person, you have to know them well. Two people I have not really cared for are Jack Palance and the late Anthony Quinn. They were absolutely rude. If a person says to me, "I don't care to take a picture," that's no big deal. Jack Nicholson turned me down. But don't be snotty about it.

AS: Is there anybody you'd still like to meet?
DR: I missed a picture with Castro. I crashed Cuba about four or five years ago, and I had it all laid out. I had nine days in Cuba, and I tried to get a picture, but I couldn't even get close. Castro played baseball. I should have gotten a picture of Tommy Lasorda and Preston Gomez, gone up to the palace and said, "Here's salutations from Tommy Lasorda and Preston Gomez." I could have gotten it.

AS: Do you buy tickets to safeguard yourself?
DR: Depends on the venue. But the thing is this; to not have the ticket torn. I will have a ticket for this game, but it will not be torn. That is proof that I made it.

AS: Do you ever plan on retiring from doing this?
DR: I'm too young to retire, for crying out loud. I'm only 73.

AS: You should write a book.
DR: I am. Right now, it's in the second fine-tuning. It's ready for the printer, and then it's going to be ready for the pictures

segment. It's going to be called, "Dion Rich—World's Greatest Gate-Crasher."

AS: What pointers would you give to those who would like to pull a Dion?

DR: One of my key bits of advice is: Always go to the bathroom before you crash, because you might get in no man's land. And another one of my biggest pieces of advice is: Always eat first. Because I know from past experience that it feels a lot better to get thrown out on a full stomach than an empty stomach.

AS: Who's going to win the Super Bowl?

DR: The Raiders. Al Davis is a friend of mine. He was with the Chargers two years before he went to Oakland. I will have an invitation to their victory party. That's guaranteed. If they don't give me one, I'm crashing it.

Postscript

After I left the Winter Olympics in Salt Lake City, I thought I was through with the Secret Service. But I wasn't. They called a couple weeks ago and requested I come down to their offices and visit with them. It was an offer I couldn't refuse.

They picked me up at my condo about 9:30 in the morning, Monday, April 7, 2003. We gathered in their conference room for three hours. There were six of us, and they really pumped me for information. They wanted to know my style, my secrets—you might even call them my tricks—to gain entrance to so many varied venues.
I shared things such as:

1. Just keep going. If you can't go in the front door, go in the side door. If you can't go in the side door, go in the back door. If you can't go in the back door, go in the kitchen door. Don't be discouraged, just keep going and you'll get in.

2. Stay in the middle of the crowd as you go through the entrance. You have less of a chance of being noticed.

3. Have a phony credential.

I went to great lengths to tell them how I "crashed" Super Bowls, World Series, All-Star Games, Kentucky Derbies, Academy Awards, to mention a few.
I also gave them some pointers:

1. It's better to use bona fide off-duty police officers rather than young, minimum wage security guards.

2.   Insist upon having photo credentials.

The Secret Service really dwelled on how I got my picture taken with President Clinton. They came back to that issue time and time again. I told them it was at a fund-raiser two years ago, before 9/11, in Beverly Hills. There was a large crowd gathered around the President. I just wiggled my way through all those bodies until I was right next to him. His Secret Service men spotted my camera, and said, "No pictures." But Clinton interrupted, and said, "No problem. A picture is okay."

As I was getting ready for the photo, I put my arm around the President, but the Secret Service quickly took my arm away. There was no touching the President.

The three people you can't touch are the president, the Queen of England and Lauren Bacall

Secret Service meeting, April 2003

All in all, the Secret Service couldn't thank me enough, and said I was extremely helpful to them. After taking me to lunch, they drove me home. When we got there they asked if they could come in and photograph some of my memorabilia, and I said, "Sure, go right ahead."

I never did figure out what they were going to do with those photographs. Perhaps they were going to take them back to the laboratory and look for clues as to how I became *The World's Greatest Gate-Crasher.*

DION'S FINAL QUOTE

"Your notoriety will be determined by

the people who acknowledge your actions."

Which one is the real Oscar?